What is Putin Doing?
Russia – Ukraine Crisis

Sanctions, Peace and Security in the 21st Century

What is Putin Doing? Russia – Ukraine Crisis

Sanctions, Peace and Security in the 21st Century

By

SARON MESSEMBE OBIA

Vij Books India Pvt Ltd
New Delhi (India)

Published by

Vij Books India Pvt Ltd
(Publishers, Distributors & Importers)
2/19, Ansari Road
Delhi – 110 002
Phones: 91-11-43596460, 91-11-47340674
Mob: 98110 94883
E-mail: contact@vijpublishing.com
Web : www.vijbooks.in

ISBN: 978-93-93499-11-0 (Paperback)

Dedicated to

Almighty God and Iya Magdaline Efamba

"You are not human until you feel someone else's pain"

\- The Buddha

Contents

ACKNOWLEDGEMENT

I hail Prof. John M. Nomikos, Director at the Research Institute for European and American Studies, Chairman, European Intelligence Academy (EIA), Dr. Daniel Ekongwe, Regional Director of Pan African Institute for Development West Africa (PAID-WA), Dr Mbua David Evelle, lecturer at the University of Buea, Brig. Gen. Pradip K. Vij and Mr. Noor Dahri, Executive Director at Islamic Theology of Counter Terrorism (ITCT) for their invaluable support for my skill as international security expert.

I am grateful to Mr Charles Ebune, Mr Obia Ranndy, Mr Carmelo Aguilera, Ms Konglim Mirabel, Modika Daniel, Ms Merilyne Ojong and Mr Alvin Odinukwe.

Finally, I appreciate the work of experts of the United Nations and European Union in the struggle for peace and security, internationally and at the regional level. However, sanctions cannot limit the new wave of war. I commend dialogue and mediation for lasting peace and security.

EXECUTIVE SUMMARY

Russian annexation of Crimea on March 19, 2014, is a violation of Article 2(4) of the United Nations (UN) Charter, 1 the Budapest Memorandum on Security Assurances, and the Helsinki Accords. It has equally been engaged in a proxy war of attrition in Donbass (Donetsk and Luhansk oblasts) within parameters fixed by the Minsk II process and has successfully inserted itself into the Syrian imbroglio. These initiatives were not fortuitous; all were planned.

Putin's goal of restoring Russia's great power is a reflection of Crimea's annexation, coupled with the past success of the VPK's military industrial research and development (R&D) 2002-2010 initiative achieved under The Reform and Development of the Defense Industrial Complex Program 2002-2006, signed by then-Prime Minister Mikhail Kasyanov in October 2001,15 and the State Armament Programme for Russia for the years 2011 to 2020, signed by then-President Dmitry Medvedev at the end of 2010.

After the annexation of the Crimean Peninsula and Sevastopol in March 2014 from Ukraine, thereby becoming two federal subjects of the Russian Federation. Despite Sanctions imposed to Russia following the invasion of Ukraine, four executive orders (E.O.s) were issued by President Obama in 2014. Legislation in response to Russian actions includes, but not limited to the following: Sergei Magnitsky Rule of Law Accountability Act of 2012 (P.L. 112-208, Title IV; 22 U.S.C. 5811 note); Support for the

Sovereignty, Integrity, Democracy, and Economic Stability of Ukraine Act of 2014, as amended (SSIDES; P.L. 113-95; 22 U.S.C. 8901 et seq.); Countering Russian Influence in Europe and Eurasia Act of 2017, as amended (CRIEEA; P.L. 115-44, Countering America's Adversaries Through Sanctions Act [CAATSA], Title II; 22 U.S.C. 9501 et seq.); Protecting Europe's Energy Security Act of 2019, as amended (PEESA; P.L. 116-92, Title LXXV; 22 U.S.C. 9526 note)

Western powers, including the EU and the U.S. imposed several restrictive measures on Russia in order to influence the Kremlin's foreign policy towards Ukraine. The theory of international economic sanctions analyses the content and application of sanctions and assesses whether the sanctions are adequate to reconfigure the geopolitical trajectory of the Russian Federation.

The strategic horizons of Russia are clearly seen in the Group of Twenty (G20) format. Moscow continues to exploit it as additional leverage to coordinate regional and global policies with China and aspiring nations cooperating at the economic and security level. The Group of Eight (G8) format, dismantled by its Western members because of the Ukrainian crisis, has, however, not exhausted its potential. The suspension of Russia's membership is not an insurmountable obstacle for Russia's pursuit of its foreign policy objectives, but to resume it sooner or later would be in everybody's interests. Russia is gradually enjoying its history as the largest land empire, as it is shaping mechanisms of regional and global governance and regulation in the world.

Chapter One

Introduction

The world has moved from war to law, to war back to law and today to war[1]. During World War I, the Bolsheviks, with Red Army support, after conquering the Ukrainian nationalist government in Kyiv, took control of the territory that became the Ukrainian Soviet Socialist Republic (UkSSR). However, Ukrainian agriculture made her enjoy relatively lenient treatment under the USSR system before the rise of Joseph Stalin. When Stalin became premier, the latter introduced farm collectivization, grain quotas, Russification, and persecution, which led to famine (the Holodomor, 1932–1933) and the deaths of about three and ten million Ukrainians.

The Russo-Ukrainian relations are not new to scholars in the field of international relations and conflict management in Europe. Russia's cultural, religious, and political heritage is linked to some areas in Ukraine. One of the most pertinent issues is that both countries share politico-religious affiliations, political parentage with the Kyivan Rus, and the Slavic world to Orthodox Christianity which began in Crimea. Just like Pakistan, the territory known as Ukraine was persistently contested and divided among competing

---

1   Dr Daniel Ekongwe lecture notes on world order at the Pan African Institute for Development West Africa (PAID-WA), Buea, Cameroon.

imperial powers, after which the western regions of Ukraine, which were controlled by Poland, were taken by Bolsheviks.

Beyond its religious significance, the history of Crimea betrays the peninsula's geopolitical and geostrategic interests. One of the significant conquest of the Russian Empire in 1774, the Crimean Peninsula was a strategic terrain which was exploited against the coalition of Great Britain, France, Sardinia, and Turkey during the Crimean War (1853–1856). Sevastopol's defence against Nazi invasion during World War II showcases Russian authority, earning the city the honorific "Hero City." There is no doubt that historical facts merge with intelligence analysis, appeal to Russia's premier that Crimea is a strategic buffer against foreign powers and that losing the peninsula would undermine Russia's status as a superpower.

With the battle for supremacy around the world, the power in Kyiv, perceive Ukraine's growing cooperation and partnerships with the EU as a strategic menace, there by imposing economic, trade, and financial reprisals. From 2007 to late 2009, Ukraine was subjected to a series of energy disputes, financial panics, and gas shortages. This period was also characterized by the Russian quest for dominance, with threatening and militarily aggression. Putin equally warned during a NATO summit in Bucharest that if Ukraine joined the alliance, it would risk losing Crimea and eastern Ukraine.

In August 2008, Russia invaded Georgia, in order to stop her NATO membership (former Soviet bloc). Russia further succeeded in securing the separatist regions of Georgia, creating a frozen conflict and effectively curtailing the prospect of NATO membership. Notably, the Black Sea Fleet based in Sevastopol, Crimea, participated in the conflict, demonstrating its criticality to Russia's efforts to maintain its supremacy and influence in the region.

Genesis of the Conflict in Ukraine

Several questions have been posed to understand the dynamics of international security in the 21st century; why the non-respect of the Westphalia treaty of 1648? Is the United Nations failing? What accounts for the fragmentation of states across the world? In analyzing the first phase (2013-2014) of the conflict in Ukraine, the genesis is structured in three phases and according to their link to each of the conflicts identified: internal conflict or wrangling, Ukraine-Russia and West-Russia.

The 'game' begins when former President of Ukraine, Viktor Fedorovych Yanukovych, discards signing an accord with the EU to deepen trade. This event indicates the existence of significant polarization within the country towards ideological and economic frameworks available in Europe, once a series of popular manifestations arise against the political decision. After the refusal to validate an accord with EU, two major conflicts arouse between Ukraine and Russia, and Russia and the West. The three of them show their interdependency until the internal conflict in Ukraine derives into a situation of low-intensity war by May 2014.

Phase 1 - Internal wrangling

The major aspect for internal wrangling in Ukraine, was President Yanukovich's resolution to back away from an agreement to further commerce with the EU, which sparked a series of popular manifestations in the main cities of the country opposing this political decision. Soon enough polarization translated into violence in the streets. The 21st of November marks the beginning of internal wrangling throughout Ukraine.

The mass media compares the events in the country to that of the Orange revolution. Critically, on the 26 of

November, the EU rejected Ukraine's proposal to begin talks simultaneously with Russia, an indicator of the existence of an underlying conflict between the West and Russia. More so, more than 100,000 people gathered at Kyiv's main plaza rejecting President Yanukovich's decision, and appealed for his resignation; which the police reacted harshly and violently on the streets and called the attention of the international community, yet to respond. However, reports revealed that, police officers were also targets. Ex-Ukrainian Interior Minister, Vitaly Zakharchenko, declared to RT ("100% sure," 2014) that during these days, 86 officers were shot at, 14 of them died, and none of the officers deployed were carrying their service weapons. From another perspective, it is relevant to note that the violence and the Ukrainian winter frost were unable to dissolve the will of the protesters on the streets, in this sense calls the attention to the fact that they stood up for so many days in the cold, without international community intervening, indicate the failing nature of international actors and organizations in the contemporary era.

The clash between superpowers delayed the talks between Ukraine and Russia, taking the situation to a different dimension, which cannot be justified today, even with sanctions imposed on Russia. After several events in Ukraine, on 23 of February, the parliamentarians agreed to name Olexander Turchynov as interim President of the country, one day after President Yanukovich was ousted from office by the Ukrainian Parliament. The agreement reached on 21 February has pointed Ukrainians quest for peace and security, as per its fourth paragraph: "Investigation into recent acts of violence will be conducted under joint monitoring from the authorities, the opposition and the Council of Europe" (Agreement on the Settlement of Crisis in Ukraine. 21 February 2014). A report by Amnesty International, in 2015 revealed that, "Violations by police, including torture and other ill treatment as well as abusive use of force during demonstrations, continued with near-total impunity for the perpetrators, while investigations into such incidents remained ineffective" (Amnesty International, 2015).

Phase 2 - External Conflicts

The first phase of the conflict was focused on internal wrangling, which introduced one of the most critical phase which appeals for modern warfare in Ukraine. The political narrative over Ukraine sphere, then the other two underlying conflicts, between Kyiv and Moscow, and the West and Russia.

1. Internal

On the 22 of February, when President Yanukovich was ousted, people in the cities of Bila Tserkva, Khmelnitsky and Zhytomyr brought down statues of Lenin. This action sparked new events, as pro-Russians stand to protect the statue of the Russian communist revolutionary in Kharkiv. The rise of new premier did not limit the events in the country, as unrest still continued in the Russian-speaking regions of the country where there is opposition to the new administration in Kyiv. Despite, BBC News ("Ukraine crisis," 2014) reports on the warning issued by interim President Turchynov, about the dangers of separatism, nothing was done by the international community. As most activists took to the streets of main cities along the country where clashes had taken placed between pro-Russians and pro-Ukrainians. Two days later, Kyiv had asked the OSCE to bring observers to the South and East of the country[2]. The government appealed for alternative ways to resolve the issue, while asking the population not to support unconstitutional activities. Among these events of heightened polarization and violence of the internal

---

2   https://www.redalyc.org/journal/927/92746462007/html//

wrangling in Ukraine, a different kind of situation began to unfold in Crimea, initiating a second curve.

2. Russia and Ukraine game

The war in Ukraine and the failure of the United Nations (UN) to bring the two parties to the table and the inadequacy of the EU. After several clashes between pro-Russians and anti-Russians, took place on the streets of Simferopol, the events in Crimea exposed a different dimension of instability taking place in the country. Moreover, when a pro-Russian command expels the local government of Crimea and took control of the capital's parliament, where they vote to approve a referendum to ask for more autonomy for the region, impulse the second phase of the crisis with the manifestation of another conflict, the one between Russia and Ukraine, which involved different interests.

Though Russia refuted involvement in the process that derived to the annexation of Crimea, in fact the first comments on the issue by the President of the Russian Federation, Vladimir Putin, were on the 4th of March, denying the presence of Russian troops in the peninsula. The premier later stated on a live TV program that Russian 'machine' had been involved in wresting Crimea from Kyiv's control, explaining that they had to take unavoidable steps, "so that events did not develop as they are currently developing in southeast Ukraine"[3]. He stated that the annexation was partly triggered by NATO expansion, explaining that:

'If NATO goes there, Russia will be pushed out from the area around the Black Sea. This is pushing out Russia from this important part of the world. Let's not be afraid of

---

3 Anischchuk, A. (2014, April 17) Putin admits Russian forces were deployed to Crimea. Reuters.Retrieved from: http://uk.reuters.com/article/2014/04/17/russiaputin-crimea-idUKL6N0N921H20140417

anything, but we should take that into account, and respond accordingly'.[4]

On the 28 of February, armed men captured airports of Belbek and Simferopol; only then, Kyiv accuses Moscow of exerting an armed invasion and occupation. The Federation Council, approves a military intervention in Ukraine, invoking the right to protect (R2P) its interests and pro-Russians. This event alerts the Ukrainian military 'machine' and stands as a warning sign to the West. The Ukrainian prime minister appeals on Russian intervention, argues that Moscow has declared war. Western powers then begin talks with Russia to lower the pressure on her 'machinery'. Meanwhile, Ukraine accelerates the pace of its diplomacy to gain support for its cause.

It's necessary to acknowledge that on the 6 of March, the Crimean Parliament decided the annexation of the peninsula to Russia and calls for a referendum for the citizens to vote. This same day, Russia sinks one of its own ships in a strategic area of the Black Sea to block the exit of Ukrainian vessels from the Crimean Peninsula. Russian government finally declared to back up Crimea if the region voted favouring the secession of Ukraine.

Meanwhile, by the 9th of March, there were clashes between Pro-Russian and anti-Russian factions in the streets of the main cities in Ukraine and the country's Prime Minister, Arseniy Yatsenyuk asked the people not to cede a single centimeter to Russia. Nevertheless, the referendum that took place in Crimea, with official data revealing more than 82% of the population of Crimea participated on the referendum, from which more than 96% voted in favour of

---

4   Gentleman, A. (2014, April 17) Putin asserts right to use force in east Ukraine. The Guardian. Retrieved from: http://www.theguardian.com/world/2014/apr/17/vladimirputin-denies-russian-forceseastern-ukraine-Kyiv

the annexation to Russia. This became a fact on the 18th of March when President Putin signed the documents changing the flag of the Crimean Peninsula.

Ukraine's immediate response to the loss of territory by signing out of the Commonwealth of Independent States (under the lead of Moscow) on the 19th of March. The latter then signed the political chapters of an agreement of association with the EU and participated in military exercises with NATO in Bulgaria. This move led the Russian Minister of Foreign Affairs, Sergey Lavrov, to suggest for the federalization of Ukraine as a means to settle the internal wrangling. On 3rd of April, the Russians remilitarized the region of Volgograd, close to the border with Ukraine. The internal conflict of Ukraine took a different dimension, with separatists movements taking control of public buildings in Donetsk and Luhansk on the 6th of April, which is attributed to a 'second wave' of a special operation held by the Russian Federation against Ukraine.

Russia and the West

The relationship between Moscow and Washington have been so good in the Trump administration, than that of other administrations. The Obama administration asked President Putin to withdraw Russian forces back to their military bases; this indicated the beginning of the second part of the second phase of the events: when a third conflict unfolded. This phase reveals how Russia imposed its interests over the conflict between Moscow and Kyiv. The discourse takes the form of a defence of Ukraine's sovereignty and territorial integrity, alleging the illegality of the referendum to vote for the secession of Crimea and later the annexation of the peninsula by Moscow, but it is the interest to put a stop to Russian influence in Eastern Europe. Some of the actors involved are NATO, Canada, Poland, OSCE, UN, EU, Switzerland and France.

On the 3rd of March, the American military machine (Pentagon) announced that, the suspension of every military tie between Washington and Moscow as a consequence of the Russian intervention in Crimea. The NATO also suspended the participation of Russia in what was going to become their first joint mission; restricting every meeting between military and civilian officers from Russia; and submitted to review every aspect of cooperation between NATO and Russia. Limiting talks only to Ambassador level officers.

Canada followed the move by expelling nine Russian military officers from the country who were invited as part of a professional exchange program, also suspended every bilateral link with its armed forces, including already planned meetings and military exercises. European Emergency Council condemned the violation of Ukraine's sovereignty and its territorial integrity. By the 8th, OSCE monitors receive warning shots for their attempt to visit the Crimean Peninsula.

Didier Burkhalter, leader of the OSCE and Switzerland's Minister of Foreign Affairs, condemned the Crimea referendum. On the 15th, Moscow vetoed a UN resolution draft that criticized the referendum about Crimea's secession. But voters approved the annexation to Russia, while the EU and NATO declared it would not recognize the results because they considered it illegal and illegitimate.

On the 17th, the US imposed economic restrictions on a Russian bank and 11 Russian citizens close to President Putin (who allegedly had participated in Crimea's annexation). NATO and the US highlighted the importance of developing a joint international response to the continuous violation of

Ukraine's sovereignty and territorial integrity[5]. Meanwhile, the EU condemned Russia for Crimea's annexation and imposed sanctions on Russian and Ukrainian citizens that participated in the process.

On the 21st, NATO's Secretary-General, Anders Fogh Rasmussen, considered the events in Ukraine as a geopolitical game-changer, for which he settled three priorities for the allies to face Russia's military aggression against Ukraine. Scholars pose several questions as to the 'game' in Ukraine and that in Afghanistan; question which all focus on sovereignty and territorial integrity as per the Westphalia treaty of 1648. But the battle for US to remain a major super power by NATO's secretary general relay on these three points; To reaffirm Allied commitment to collective defence; Strengthened support to Ukraine and the wider region; "And to make clear that we can no longer do business as usual with Russia"[6].

On the 24th, Russia sanctions 13 Canadian government officials as a reprisal for similar measures implemented by that country. On the 27th, UN's General Assembly approves a resolution stating that Crimea's referendum is illegal. NATO advanced by an increase of military planes in Baltic States, followed the suspension of every type of military and civilian cooperation with Russia, and asked Generals and Admirals of the Alliance to propose ideas for the defence of members in Eastern Europe. Jane's published satellite images, which indicated Russian expansion in Belgorod (located 40 km from Ukrainian border), and she began military exercises in the Volgograd area (385 km from Luhansk, Ukraine).

---

5   https://www.redalyc.org/journal/927/92746462007/html//

6   Rasmussen, A. F. (2014, March) Address by the NATO Secretary General. Presented at the Brussels Forum conference. Retrieved from: http://www.nato.int/nato_static_fl2014/assets/audio/audio_2014_03/20140321_140321a.mp3

Following NATO breach relations with Russia on April 1st, Russia called its Ambassador to the entity, indicating it has changed its narrative to the events in Ukraine. NATO's deputy Secretary General, Ambassador Alexander Vershbow, revealed that Europe's strategic environment has changed:

"for 20 years, the security of the Euro-Atlantic region has been based on the premise that we do not face an adversary to our East. This premise is now in doubt"[7] .

Phase 3 – Secession in Eastern Ukraine

The annexation of Crimea by Russia is considered as a failed accomplishment, the internal wrangling in Ukraine revamps with the spread of separatism, particularly in the Eastern regions of the country. The separatist movement (secessionists ideas) in Ukraine starting on the 6th of April is perceived as a 'second wave' of Russian activity against Kyiv. While Ukraine and the West accused Russia's involvement in the 'game', Moscow refutes and indicated that the crisis in Ukraine "is to be blamed on those who organized the state coup in Kyiv"[8]. Although Moscow has denied its involvement with the separatists movements that emerge after the Crimean issue, there is not enough evidence to accuse Moscow. From a realist perspective, Eastern Ukraine is an area of Russian geopolitical interest, and strategic in case of any war in Europe. The West and Ukraine understand that Russia has to be part of a solution. Sanctions would not solve the situation, but rather create more casualties.

---

7   Vershbow, A. (2014, April) A new strategic reality in Europe. Presented at the 21st International Conference on Euro-Atlantic Security, Krakow, Poland. Retrieved from: http://www.nato.int/cps/en/ natolive/opinions_108889.htm

8   Kyiv says ready for dialogue withUkraine's federalization supporters. (2014, May 8) Tass. Retrieved from:http://tass.ru/en/world/730860

The spirit of secession and internal wrangling

Until the first days of May, the level of intensity of the internal conflict oscillates between high levels of violence to a mid-level of polarization, taking note that there are many consecutive high points by the end of April.

On the 6th of April separatist groups took control of public buildings of cities in Donetsk, Luhansk and Kharkiv. The next day, pro-Russians announced the formation of the Republic of Donetsk, called for a referendum to be held on the 11th of May, to ask for the annexation to Russia and calls Moscow to send peacekeepers to warrant the feasibility of the process, but none of these occurred. President of Ukraine, Oleksander Turchynov announced prohibition to perform separatist activities in the country, followed by security forces (from Kyiv) antiterrorist operation in Kharkiv.

On the 17th of April the Geneva Accord was signed by representatives from Russia, EU and Ukraine to lower tensions in the East. Despite the agreement, violence continues; separatists did not participate on the arrangements so they did not comply returning public buildings nor with the disarmament. A group of rebels took hostage eight European military observers (one was liberated three days later, the rest by the 3rd of May). The mayor of Kharkiv witnessed an assassination attempt.

It was revealed that, at least 40 pro-Russians dead in street clashes in Odessa, most of them were burnt alive or suffocated to death in the local House of Trade Unions, "many of those who managed to escape the fire were then brutally beaten by armed men"[9]. On 2 May, a military operation took place in Kramatorsk; there were fierce combats against separatists

---

9   Odessa slaughter: How vicious mob burnt anti-govt activists alive. (2014, May 3) RT. Retrieved from: https://www.rt.com/news/156592- odessa-activists-burnt-alive/

in an effort to recover Slavyansk (in the region of Donetsk). For the first time during the crisis under scrutiny, a conflict reaches the level of war. Fighting continued at least through the 6th, according to The Guardian ("Ukraine is close," 2014) this day the German foreign minister declared that Ukraine is a few steps away from a military confrontation[10].

On the 11th referendums about the autonomy of provinces were held in Luhansk and Donetsk, the following day the Popular Republic of Donetsk formally requests the annexation to the Russian Federation. Struggles continue as the EU and Ukraine rejected the referendum, while Russia respected its result. On the 17th the intensity reaches a mid-level of violence when there is a roundtable on national unity in Kharkiv among separatist's occupations. However, this was only a parenthesis, because by the 22nd the conflict increases its intensity again reaching a low level of war, which is maintained the following days. President Putin believes Ukraine had descended into full-scale civil war, but refuted Moscow was behind acts involving pro-Russia separatists (as cited in "Russia's Vladimir," 2014).

1. Ukraine - Russia.

Amid accusations from Ukraine on the alleged participation of Russia in the Eastern separatist movement, Moscow states that if it is attacked it will have to respond. In this regard, foreign minister Lavrov declares, "We will keep doing everything possible to consecutively protect the interests of Russian diasporas both in Ukraine and in other states"[11].

---

10 Ukraine is close to war, warns German minister. (2014, May 6) The Guardian. Retrieved from: http://www.theguardian.com/world/2014/may/06/ukraine-claims-30-prorussia-separatists-killed

11 Pochuev, M. (2014, April 14) Lavrov: Moscow to do its best to protect Russians in Ukraine. Tass. Retrieved from: http://tass.ru/en/russia/727738 also Cristián Faundes (2016) An analysis of the crisis in Ukraine, and its three conflicts (21 of November 2013, through 23 of May 2014)1 Revista de

Accordingly, Russia and later Ukraine deployed forces close to the frontier, heightening tensions. Russia declares its conformity with the Geneva Accords, accuses Kyiv of violating it (on 21st of April) and states on the 24th that Ukrainian authorities commit a crime if they use the army against their own people in the East. On the other hand, that same day Ukraine's acting President, Oleksander Turchynov, said in a national address that "Russia is supporting terrorism in our country"[12]. On the 23rd, Russia begins military drills near the border with Ukraine, Russian Federation, Defence Minister, Sergei Shoigu, declared it was on response to "Ukraine's military machine" and NATO exercises in Eastern Europe (as cited in Vasovic & Anishchuk, 2014).

It should be noted that on the 7th of May, President Putin appealed to Kyiv to stop the security operation held in the East. Instead the Ukrainian government revealed the deployment of 15.000 troops by the border with Russia. On the 11th Moscow opened a voting station for Ukrainians, the next day an official statement delivered from the Russian president's press service tensions the relationship once again because of an alleged interference in Ukraine's internal matters by supporting the regions' autonomy process:

Moscow respects the expression of will of the population of the Donetsk and Luhansk regions and proceeds on the basis that the implementation of the results of the referendums will be carried out in a civilized way, without any relapse of violence, through dialogue between representatives of Kyiv, Donetsk and Luhansk. ("Moscow respects," 2014)

Relaciones Internacionales, Estrategia y Seguridad, vol. 11, no. 2, pp. 137-159, 2016 Universidad Militar Nueva Granada

12   Vasovic, A. & Anishchuk, A. (2014, April 25) Ukraine forces kill up to five rebels; Russia starts drill near border. Reuters. Retrieved from: http://www. reuters.com/article/2014/04/25/us-ukrainecrisis-idUSBREA3L11A20140425

On the 19th, the Kremlin criticizes Ukraine's military campaign in the Southeast as well as the process for a constitutional reform because of an alleged lack of transparency. Russia initiates the retreat of military forces from Rostov, Belgorod and Bryansk to their permanent bases. Kyiv welcomes President Putin's statement that the Kremlin will cooperate with authorities elected in the Ukrainian polls (held on the 25th). But events will later change because of the new leadership.

1. The West and Russia.

The tension between the West and Russia tends to lower initially along this phase reaching a mid to low level of polarization, from the 8th of April through the 22nd. Afterwards, the intensity of the conflict heightens, oscillating from a mid-level of polarization to a low level of violence, until the 19th of May. By the end of the period studied the relationship reaches a low level of polarization with events occurred the 21st.

The 'game' in Ukraine may seem paradoxical, but real because of the quest for supremacy and geostrategic reasons. While the NATO's Secretary General warns Russia not to interfere in Ukraine's internal affairs (8 of April), President Obama requested President Putin to end support to pro-Russian separatists (14 of April) and President Putin urges President Obama to prevent a bloodshed in the country (15 of April). Its necessary to reveal that, on the 18th both parties adhered to the Geneva Accords, but the Kremlin made it very clear it will not accept further sanctions against Russia.

International relations as defined as a brutal 'game' painted in white, could reveal the patterns of some actors, when US Vice President Joe Biden personally brought to Kyiv a new package of nonlethal aid (including medical supplies and helmets), then appealing on Russia to stop supporting "men hiding behind masks"[13]. Russian Prime Minister, Dmitry Medvedev, replies stating that Russia is "ready for unfriendly steps" (as cited in Smith, 2014_b).

Moreover, US troops arrived at Eastern Europe, initiating a rotatory presence in the region to perform training exercises in Poland, Lithuania, Latvia and Estonia; Dutch fighters intercepted two Russian bombardiers in its airspace; and Russian military units initiated drills by the border with Ukraine for geostrategic purposes. As previously noted, the latter was triggered as a response to Ukraine's deployment and NATO's exercises in Europe. The protient-allaince (West) and some other states decided to impose new sanctions against Russia; despite these sanctions the stock market in Moscow responded by raising its value. President Putin "responded by threatening to reconsider Western participation in energy deals" in the country[14]. But US Secretary of State, John Kerry, declares that "Today, Russia seeks to change the security landscape of eastern and central Europe", adding that whatever path Russia chooses, "the United States and our allies will stand together in our defence of Ukraine" (as cited in Tribune wire reports, 2014).

Russia activates a nationwide military exercise simulating a nuclear attack. Leaders of the Collective Security Treaty Organization observed the drills with President Putin, it included the launching of intercontinental missiles from the Northeastern territories and from two nuclear submarines from the Pacific Fleet and the Northern Fleet. Moscow will

---

13 Smith, A. (2014_a, April 22) Biden Slams Russia: Stop Supporting'Men Hiding Behind Masks'. NBCNews. Retrieved from: http://www.nbcnews. com/storyline/ukrainecrisis/biden-slams-russia-stopsupporting-men-hiding-behindmasks-n86416

14 Tribune wire reports (2014, April 30) Ukraine forces in 'full military readiness' un case of Russia invasion.Chicago Tribune. Retrieved from:http://articles. chicagotribune.com/2014-04-30/news/chiukraine-crisis-20140430_1_ Ukraine-forces-eastern-ukraineoleksander-turchinov

later appeal for a Russia NATO Council session about the sharp deterioration of the situation in Ukraine (a week later there was still no date for the summit). In order to understand the genesis of the conflict in Ukraine it was necessary to observe separately each one of the interacting conflicts: the internal one, another between Ukraine and Russia, and the other with Moscow and the West.

CHAPTER TWO

THEORETICAL FRAMEWORKS AND RUSSIAN WARFARE

Moscow is considered as one of the dominant 'super power' in the world, and is oftentimes considered tyrant, because of the Slavic Orthodox civilization. The cleavage between Western and Slavic Orthodox civilizations, emerge from Ukraine, based on the historical link of Russian nation to the Kyivan Rus' Empire. The division between the Latin Church and Orthodoxy was exemplified by the 1472 marriage of the Grand Prince of Moscow Rus Ivan III to Sophia Paleologue, aspirant to[15] the throne of the Byzantine Empire, at the recommendation of Pope Paul II in an unsuccessful attempt to merge the two civilizations. Even after the union, Russian supremacy and civilization reveal Moscow as the "third Rome," following Constantinople. Ivan III began to refer to himself as Tsar, the Russian derivation of Caesar. Vladimir Putin's interest and intervention in Ukraine emanated from these deep roots and, more recently, from the dramatic experiences of the Soviet Union never to happen again.

In 1654, Cossack hetman Bohdan Khmelnytsky signed the Treaty of Pereyaslav, allying the Cossack people of Ukraine and the Russian Empire against Poland. But in 1704, another

---

15 https://www.jhuapl.edu/Content/documents/ARIS_LittleGreenMen.pdf

Cossack hetman, Ivan Mazepa, threw in his lot with Charles XII of Sweden against the tsar. Centuries later, these two figures elicit both praise and condemnation from Ukrainian nationalists on the one hand and the pro-Russian population on the other. Mazepa's image decorates the Ukrainian ten-hryvnia note, but in Kyiv a street named in his honour was renamed under Viktor Yanukovych's administration, and Mazepa remains anathematized by the Russian[16] Orthodox Church.

Russian and Soviet narratives point to the Treaty of Pereyaslav to illustrate the perpetual union of the Ukrainian and Russian peoples. Ukraine's borders stabilized as the territory of the Ukrainian Soviet Socialist Republic (SSR) was expanded at the end of World War II to encompass territories taken from Poland and Romania[17]. The makeup of Ukraine's population also shifted dramatically after World War II as millions of Russians moved into Ukraine to rebuild and industrialize the region, a process that shaped the region into the economic engine of the USSR. Propaganda stressed the unity of Ukraine and Russia on the basis of centuries of claimed historical precedent. In 1954, during a celebration of the Treaty of Pereyaslav, Russian premier Nikita Khrushchev transferred the Russian-majority Crimean Peninsula to the Ukrainian SSR, certain that Kyiv and Moscow[18] would be perpetually bound together. Recent Russian propaganda points to the artificial nature of Ukraine's borders and decries the mixture of West-leaning populations with pro-Russian eastern Slavs.

---

16 https://nsarchive.gwu.edu/media/16170/ocr

17 ibid

18 https://briandcolwell.com/4ir-geopolitics-investing-in-russias-asymmetri-cal-warfare/

Russia has reconfigured her system to adapt to the new world order, there by developing a strategy to deal with states and regions around the periphery of the Federation. The nonmilitary factors are politics, diplomacy, economics, finance, information, and intelligence, meanwhile, in the information domain, there is the use of cyber warfare and propaganda. However, most scholars argue that, there have been a persistent denial of Russian operations, use of unidentified local and Russian agents and the start of military activity without war declaration; actions appear to be spontaneous actions of local troops/militias.

Russian's 'game' in Crimea and eastern Ukraine in 2013–2014 demonstrated a radical departure from the paradigm of twentieth-century conventional warfare and a new strategy by Moscow after the dissolution of the Soviet Union in the Baltic states (1990–1991), Transnistria (1990–1992), Chechnya and Dagestan (1994–2009), and the Russo-Georgian War of 2008.

The Russian conquest or annexation of Crimea and Kyiv's acquiescence in greater autonomy for eastern Ukraine marvelled the West, raising fears that Russia's success in Ukraine may lead to further aggression in the Baltic states, Moldova, or Poland. Moscow's agenda vary from outright annexation but for geostrategic reasons which might emanate in the future in the quest for some states to maintain their supremacy while exploiting Ukraine as buffer.

Moreover, Russia's unconventional warfare techniques challenge the provisions of Article 5 of the NATO Charter because the treaty invokes collective security in response to "armed attack" by another power. With focus on Ukraine, Moscow denied involvement and employed proxies and deception to obviate the stigma attached to a conventional armed invasion.

Drawing from Samuel Huntington's Clash of Civilizations, the nature and course of conflicts among nations is based on civilizations. He out pin eight such civilizations, which involve but are not limited to; Western, Islamic, Confucian, and Japanese civilizations. Nonetheless, the piece provides a clear narrative on the Iran-Iraq war, and Operation Desert Storm, which is a description of the conflict between Western and Islamic civilizations. Neither did the international community perceive the growing rift between the successor state to the Soviet Union, now the Russian Federation and the West.

THE RUSSIAN THEORY

Information Warfare

Russian information warfare techniques emanate from the genius of Igor Panarin and Alexandr Dugin, drawing from an amalgamation of methods evolved within the Soviet Union (with roots as far back as tsarist Russia) and strategic developments in response to scrutiny of Western (especially American) operations in the twenty-first century. The revitalized doctrine or spetz propaganda, is taught in the Military Information and Foreign Languages Department of the Military University of the Ministry of Defence to military personnel, intelligence operatives, journalists, and diplomats are being trained. The doctrine specifies that an information campaign is multidisciplinary and includes politics, economics, social dynamics, intelligence, diplomacy, psychological operations, communications, and cyber warfare.

In general, Russian information warfare aims for Russian-speaking diaspora that fragmented into the various post-Soviet era states. It's a crusade, appealing to the masses, both home and abroad, and conditioning them for the civilizational struggle between Russia's Eurasian culture and the West. The theory is military and nonmilitary, technological and social. Information warfare is likewise the chief tool with which the state achieves diplomatic leverage and attains its foreign policy goals. It advocates for Russian civilization, through coordinated manipulation of the entire information domain (such as; newspapers, television, Internet websites, and blogs). Russian operatives attempt to create a virtual reality in the conflict zone that either influences perceptions or replaces actual ground truth with pro-Russian fiction.

Military Forces

Russia reconfigured her national and military strategy in the mid-2000s, in order to boost the military services. The development of the new strategy was to face new challenges abroad, and around the Russian Federation's periphery.

The consequent "new-look" reforms aimed at a structured, professional, and modernized force in order to combat emerging challenges included international terrorism, organized crime, proliferation of weapons of mass destruction, and regional conflict.

In a bid to maintain is 'figure' as a super power, Russia advocated to lead, and integrate Commonwealth of Independent States (CIS) military security efforts (through the Collective Security Treaty Organization) while maintaining order along the periphery. Exploiting the Collective Security Treaty Organization and the Shanghai Cooperation Organization, Russia sought to influence nearby states to reject NATO and the EU in favour of close relations with Moscow. However, in 2011, Putin succeeded in pressuring peripheral states to join the Eurasian Economic Union (EEU) rather than associate with the EU, which help to control and protect Russian diasporas abroad.

More so, Putin saw NATO as major menace to Russian plans, though no eventual invasion from the West was mapped out, Russia foresaw that NATO and the EU, along with Western nongovernmental organizations, would attempt to intervene within peripheral states to turn them against Moscow. Putin adopted a new strategy by cooperating with Beijing and pursued a lucrative deal to supply China with natural gas over the ensuing decades.

These changes in strategic outlook required changes in the military machine. The 2008 Russo–Georgian War highlighted shortcomings throughout the Ministry of Defence and the armed forces in general. The war made Russia to rethink on tactics and equipment for larger conventional war, because the 'game' seem challenging at the time.

The military machine, therefore, sought a professionalize and modernized force capable of conducting more effective operations, especially on the periphery. Key issues were command and control, personnel policies, training and readiness, equipment modernization, and the retention of nuclear deterrence. To streamline command and control, new-look reforms organized the military into four geographic joint military districts: the Western, Central, Southern, and Eastern Military Districts. Divisions and regiments were eliminated and replaced by a brigade system for the Army, while the Air Force reorganized into airbases. 33 Navy units came under the command of military districts.

The Russian Army organized eighty-five brigades through 2009, including forty combined-arms brigades as well as specialized brigades for missiles, artillery, rocket artillery, air defence, engineers, electronic warfare, reconnaissance, and special forces. To boost recruitment, the government increased pay, improved military housing, and launched a comprehensive public information campaign designed to inspire patriotism and respect for military service.

It is necessary to reiterate that, by 2008, most of the airborne forces were professional soldiers (called contract soldiers). Despite the high remuneration, Putin's administration saw the value of professionalizing the military and replacing conscripts with contract soldiers. The reveals the tenacity of and tactics (contract) soldiers in Ukraine. Most Russian soldiers were equipped with the "Ratnik" Future Soldier Individual Equipment Gear which help protect against small arms and the exploitation of a variety of subsystems, including reconnaissance, navigation, night optics, and communications.

In practice Russian Army Brigades do not deploy as whole organizations. Instead, operational commanders task organize Battalion Tactical Groups (BTGs) capable of independent combined-arms combat missions. In the summer of 2014, at least thirteen BTGs and elements of five SPETSNAZ units camped on the Ukrainian border. The main military operations in Ukraine were commanded through Russia's Southern Military District with its headquarters in Rostov-on-Don. This command has responsibility for the Caucasus and southern Russia, as well as the Black Sea and Caspian Fleets. Per treaty provisions the Russians had forces positioned in Crimea, primarily used to secure the port of Sevastopol. The following units were known or suspected to have been involved in operations or to have been preparing for operations in Crimea, eastern Ukraine, some of these forces were but are not limited to:

- ➤ 18th Detached Yevpatorian Red Banner Guard Motorized Rifle Brigade (from the Chechen Republic)
  - 1st Mechanized Battalion (also known as Vostok)

- ➢ 31st Air Assault Brigade (Airborne Forces, Ulyanovsk)

- ➢ 76th Guards Air Assault Division (Airborne Forces, Pskov)

- ➢ 106th Guards Airborne Division (Airborne Forces, Tula)

- ➢ 98th Guards Airborne Division (Airborne Forces, Ivanova)

- ➢ 7th Guards Airborne Division (Airborne Forces, Novorossiysk)

- ➢ 22nd SPETSNAZ Brigade (GRU, Krasnodar Krai)

- ➢ 45th Detached Reconnaissance Regiment (Moscow)

- ➢ Black Sea Fleet (Sevastopol)

  - • 810th Naval Infantry Brigade

  - • Kuban Cossacks

SPETSNAZ

Russian SPETSNAZ are irregular forces that operate covertly, providing the Russian government plausible deniability. They are elements of the military, intelligence, and security services. The SPETSNAZ-GRU (military intelligence) were involved in the annexation of Crimea. SPETSNAZ from the various services have different roles. Those in the FSB are tasked with counter-terrorism and protecting the constitution. They are divided into three groups: (1) Group Alpha; (2) Group Vympel; and (3) the Special Purpose Service. Alpha is involve in counter-terrorism, violent extremism and hostage rescue. Vympel is made up of strategic thinkers, with mission penetration, sabotage, and assassination. They use their skill sets to "red team" or test Russian security infrastructure.

Russia's use of SPETSNAZ evolved since its involvement in Georgia in 2008. In Crimea and eastern Ukraine, SPETSNAZ operated in a clandestine manner, with their faces masked and wearing nondescript military clothing that bore no information identifying their unit. These infamous little green men appeared during the decisive seizures or buildings and facilities, only to disappear when associated militias and local troops arrived to consolidate the gains. In this way they provided a measure of deniability, however superficial or implausible for Moscow. There is no doubt that Ukraine was alrady infiltrated before the start of the 'game', by Russia SPETSNAZ agents recruited from among the local populations, including pro-Russian nationalists, minorities, and political dissidents. When deployed, agents initially confine their efforts to political agitation and other non-kinetic methods aimed at creating a political environment favourable to Russian policies.

Russian Information Warfare in Ukraine

Russian information operations (IO) include the use of cyberwarfare. Its evident that the world is experiencing a new wave of war, that battle is cyber. Russia has taken a different shift with computer network operations feature attacks aimed at disrupting enemy infrastructure and command. Though, the Russian prelude to its 2008 conflict in Georgia, Crimea's landline, Internet, and mobile services were nearly eliminated. Hacktivists using the names Cyber Berkut and Ukraine Anonymous fought back, attacking Russian government sites and the Russia Today news agency.

Igor Panarin's thinking on Russian information warfare likely influenced Putin's strategy in Ukraine. In March 2014 Panarin commented on the Crimean 'game' and emphasize on the careful preparation of the information environment, Russia was able to obviate a more violent scenario. He further compared to the West after the performance with operations in 2008. He likewise praised what he termed "the valor of Berkut"—a reference to the Ukrainian secret police organization officially disestablished by the Kyiv government in the wake of the organization's alleged massacres of protesters. The Crimean branch of Berkut was subsequently absorbed into the Russian Ministry of Internal Affairs. Vladimir Putin was hail for the Crimean success, base on how he centralized the control of all the key political, economic, financial, military, intelligence, and information tools.

Panarin accused the West (the United States in particular) of instigating Euromaidan in Ukraine. On the basis of that premise, he views the conflict as a battle between the US-led coalition and Russia, rather than as a spontaneous domestic movement in western Ukraine. He predicts the imminent collapse of the "American–British" empire that has dominated modern history and its replacement by a large coalition of powers stretching from Egypt to China and dominated by Russia. In its new role as the leader of a multipolar world, Russia's three pillars of power will be spirituality, state power, and cyber-sovereignty.

Alexandr Dugin acknowledges that the country contains both ethnic Russians and pro-Russian populations on the one hand and West-leaning Europeans on the other. He regards the country as an artificial contrivance that inappropriately combined these two groups within a common border. Washington, he claims, is intent on pushing the divide between the two groups to the east—indeed, to the very border of Russia. Instead, Moscow must dominate that struggle through a vigorous information campaign and push the divide westward.

In Crimea, Russian spetz propaganda developed the theme that pro-Russian intervention was necessary to save the people from succumbing to "Banderivtsy and fascists from the Maidan." When necessary, Russian information warfare must include the military dimension. But both Panarin and Dugin prescribe a paradigm of military operations that is utterly different from that of the massive Russian armies of World War II.

In the Crimean operation, unidentified Russian military personnel entered the conflict region and preempted the adversary by rapidly occupying decisive points airports, media outlets, and other key infrastructure. Armed but not wearing uniforms, the Russian agents provided Moscow with deniability if not plausible deniability. The pro-Western press called the intruders little green men, but Dugin refers to them as "nice men"—citing their politeness and their diplomatic withdrawal once an area was secured. The goal is the very essence of Sun Tzu's "winning without fighting" ideal. In Crimea, it worked. In eastern Ukraine, it fell short and led to bloodshed.

Russian proponents of information warfare are not shy about sharing some of the salacious details of the operations in Crimea and eastern Ukraine. One pundit applauded the Russians' use of blackmail, psychological manipulation, and threats of nuclear war. But what makes these acts justifiable in the eyes of their champions is that they are defensive in nature. Each of the information warfare pundits portrays Russia's operations as reactions to American provocation. Because the West is victimizing Russia, everything becomes permissible in the pursuit of "true justice."

The myth of conflict resolution and alternative resolution in the 21st century

Resolution (March 16–19)

During conflict resolution, military operations reach their zenith with decisive defeat of any armed adversaries. Once the political objectives have been secured, leaders then transition to the next phase restoration of peace as a way of signaling a successful resolution. In just over three weeks of conflict, the Russians had achieved the surrender of all 190 Ukrainian bases in Crimea without firing a shot.

On March 16, the interim Crimean government held a referendum concerning secession from Ukraine and annexation into Russia. They announced that some 97 percent of the Crimean population supported such a move—a seeming impossibility, given the ethnic and language distribution on the peninsula. Two days later, Vladimir Putin signed a bill to absorb Crimea into the Russian Federation. In response the government of Ukraine, the EU, the G7, and the United States all stated that they would not recognize the results of the illegal referendum. The Venice Commission likewise ruled it illegal. On March 19, three hundred Crimean "self-defence" troops, likely led by Russian agents, stormed the headquarters of the Ukrainian Navy in Sevastopol and briefly detained Rear Admiral Sergey Gaiduk. Ukraine's troops departed without violence, and the Russian flag was raised over captured installations. The same day officials in Kyiv announced plans to pull twenty-five thousand Ukrainian troops out of Crimea and declared their break with the CIS.

The bold gamble appeared to pay off. Western powers responded with threats of further sanctions, but they simultaneously called on Russia to "pull back its troops" rather than insisting on a return to Ukrainian sovereignty over Crimea. Even Kyiv seemed quickly distracted by events in eastern Ukraine, and the Crimean annexation seemingly became a fait accompli.

Restoration of Peace (March 19–31)

On March 31, 2014, Russian prime minister Dmitry Medvedev visited Crimea and promised substantial economic aid, marking the beginning of the restoration of peace phase in Crimea. Tensions were quickly reduced in the region, and

Russian business leaders acted quickly to help integrate the region into the Russian economy. At the same time, leaders in Russia, Ukraine, and the West turned their attention to matters in eastern Ukraine, effectively acquiescing toward events in Crimea.

Russian unconventional warfare and Moscow's innovative approaches to IO largely succeeded in the recent annexation of Crimea. Nonetheless, Russia's intervention in eastern Ukraine experienced difficulties, leading to an extended conflict. While the current outcome for the Russians is mixed, it is clear that Russian leaders have absorbed the painful lessons of their post-Cold War setbacks, most notably those in Georgia in 2008. Over time they have observed and adjusted to American moves during the color revolutions and the 2010 Arab Spring. By viewing US foreign policy initiatives through the lens of geopolitics, Russian neoconservatives have embraced an aggressive foreign policy designed to reverse the losses associated with the collapse of the Soviet Union, especially along the Russian periphery. Driven by a desire to roll back Western encroachment into the Russian sphere of influence, the current generation of siloviki have crafted a multidisciplinary art and science of unconventional warfare. Capitalizing on deception, psychological manipulation, and domination of the information domain, their approach represents a notable threat to Western security interests.

A critical first step toward confronting modern Russian information warfare is to develop an understanding of its character and conduct. In conventional warfare, defenders learn to anticipate the likely "avenues of approach" that an attacking army might use. Similarly, nations and regions, particularly those on the periphery of the Russian Federation, can learn to anticipate Moscow's next steps in the use of unconventional warfare and its likely implications. When Western governments are knowledgeable of the broad range of capabilities associated with this new threat— including the use of agents, imported paramilitaries, deception, intimidation, and bribery; infiltration of political groups and government services; and persistent denial—they can fortify vulnerable sectors of society, including the media, religious organizations, political parties, and government agencies.

Chapter Three

European Union And US Sanctions

The rule of the 'game' has changed in the 21st century, with the fragmentation of states, expansionism, cyberattacks, breach of international and regional territorial demarcations and cyberwarfare. International Relations scholars view, economic sanctions as strategic policy tool which are implemented to influence other countries' foreign policy actions or coercing them into achieving the result that favours the country that initially imposed the sanctions.

According to Galtung (1967), sanctions are policy initiated by one or more international actors or organizations (UN, EU and NATO) against others (countries considered to be violators of norms or aggressor) with either or both of two purposes: to punish the state by depriving them of some value and make the state to comply with certain norms that actors or international organizations deem important. However, Galtung insists on the concept of "vulnerability," as sanctions must put pressure upon a weaker actor in order to be successful.

Economic sanctions include, but are not limited to, retaliatory tariffs in trade disputes, embargoes on a number of targeted goods, and asset seizure of entrepreneurs (Rowe, 2010). However, economic sanctions in the 21st century do not always succeed in achieving policy objectives. For

32

instance, expelling Russia from the human rights council of the UN, simply means the country can carry out any human security activity and would not be sanctioned, as the country is no longer part of the council.

Moreover, Doxey (1983: 274), proposes some features to which sanctions must adhere; for example, they must relate to a set of norms and rules and must be applicable and carry certain negative implications, regardless of whether the power is symbolic or real. For example, sanctions levied on Russia in 2014 was a façade, because of the activities of other superpowers in other countries like, Syria, and Afghanistan. More so, many scholars, including but not limited to Van Bergeijk (1989), Pape (1997), Baldwin and Page (1998) and Early (2015) out pin that, these sanctions have not been effective, and one will quick pose that, the UN, NATO and EU are political organizations.

The non-respect of the Westphalia treaty of 1648, remains one of the major menace of the new world order. Weiss (1999), reveals three possible reasons: unlike in the Cold War period, states today have bigger interests in interfering in internal affairs, resulting in a change of sovereignty notion among countries and paving the way for international organizations (the United Nations (UN), the EU) to intervene in the name of human rights. Secondly, the concept of security no longer applies solely to the military but also encompasses socio-economic, humanitarian and environmental facets. Last, but not least, countries refrain from paying the cost of military intervention and rather resort to economic sanctions[19].

Pape (1997) doubts that economic sanctions could become a reliable alternative to military force and holds that

---

19   Efe Sivişthe Crimean Annexation Crisis And Its Economic Consequences: Eu Sanctions, U.S. Sanctions And Impacts On The Russian Economy. Marmara Journal Of European Studies •Volume 27 •No: 1•2019

the main reason sanctions fail is due to the non-existence of fragile states among modern countries. Pape claims that the expectation of international cooperation will enhance the impact of sanctions is based on two dubious premises namely, that the greater cooperation only increases the economic punishment, and that the increased punishment will make a state concede. Furthermore, Baldwin and Page (1998) perceive economic sanctions to on equal footing with other foreign policy instruments, such as coercive diplomacy, propaganda or military operations that represent a constituent part of a broader framework of sanctions that are available to this day.

Sanctions are often used as a complementary measure along with other existing diplomatic tools. Kirshner (1998) argues that economic sanctions, which are designed to punish a state and change its behaviour are implemented for additional reasons, one of which is signalling. Sanctions can signal to a friend or foe that the imposer of sanctions will take steps to counter a particular action, as well as it can provide a moral support to opposition groups or serve as a warning to others contemplating similar actions.

The nature and type of sanctions are gradually developing in accordance with a shift in the understanding of modern warfare that scarcely includes military intervention but is rather focused on political, financial or diplomatic superiority. In this respect, countries are more likely to use "smart" sanctions that target the financial resources of another country, its business activity or economic restrictions (Smeets, 2018: 2). The use of sanctions by one actor against another can be seen as a struggle for power on the international arena, during which the actor that imposes the sanctions is usually perceived as "strong", whereas the actor that is being sanctioned bears the connotation of the "weak" one. Although often used by strong actors against weak ones, the economic sanctions are not only limited to this power ratio as they are put too much wider use (Resiman and Stevick, 1998: 88). For example, after the annexation of Crimea by the Russian Federation annexed Crimea, the sanctions related to Ukraine-Russia confrontation entered in the force, following the then President Obama's national emergency to tackle Russian foreign policy moves in Ukraine, which they considered to undermine democratic processes in the country and threaten peace, security and stability in the region (Department of Treasury, 2016: 3).

During the past decade, international and regional security have been under menace, of terrorist organizations, pro-secessionist, and geostrategic movements by other states. In the bid to combat these increasing menace, US established executive Orders, for the implementation of certain sanctions in accordance with the U.S. Sanctions Act and government agencies. Russia is one of the major super powers that have been issued series of executive orders against her behavior with respect to Ukraine, as well as, financial and economic sanctions that the country has to bear following the annexation of Crimea.

The US went further to extend the executive orders to individuals (Chelsea club former president), Russian government officials, government agencies and companies which they deemed associated with the development of the existing situation on the ground. The Executive Orders are as follows (U.S. Department of State):

Executive Order 1360 of 6 March 2014 authorizes sanctions on individuals and entities responsible for violating the sovereignty and territorial integrity of Ukraine, as well as for illegally acquiring assets that belonged to the Ukrainian people. The sanctions also impose travel bans on individuals and officials that are believed to be indirectly or directly involved in the situation on the ground in the Crimean Peninsula.

Executive Order 13661 of 17 March 2014 broadened the spectrum of the national emergency that was previously stipulated in Executive Order 1360. The U.S. extended the list of persons that contributed to the situation in Ukraine, mainly referring to those officials and senior officials in the Government of the Russian Federation who have acted in such a way to undermine the democratic processes, Ukraine's territorial integrity, sovereignty and the independence of the Ukrainian people, along with their contribution to the theft of the country's assets.

The Executive Order of 20 March 2014 entitled "Blocking Property of Additional Persons Contributing to the Situation in Ukraine," again broadened the sanctions that were previously announced in the two previous Executive Orders, Executive Order 13660 and Executive Order 13661, respectively.

Similar to the previous Orders, this Executive Order found that the policies of the Russian Federation undermine democratic processes and institutions in Ukraine; threaten its peace, security, stability, sovereignty, and territorial integrity, and thereby constitute a menace to the national security and foreign policy of the United States (The White House, 2014b).

Unlike previous Orders, with Executive Order 13685, the U.S. expanded the scope of the diplomatic and financial measures as a result of Russia's actions against Ukraine, including the suspension of credit finance encouraging exports to Russia and finance for economic development projects in Russia. It also prohibits the provision, exportation, or re-exportation of goods, services (not including financial services), or technology in support of exploration or production for deepwater, the Arctic offshore, or shale projects that have the potential to produce oil in the Russian Federation (Executive Order 13685 of December 19, 2014).

During the visit of Ukrainian President Poroshenko to Washington on 20 June 2017, the Treasury Department announced the extension of the sanctions, to include more than three dozen additional individuals and organizations that are directly or indirectly connected with worsening the situation in Ukraine and Crimean Peninsula. In addition, Treasury Secretary Steven Mnuchin noted that there will be no lift of sanctions until Russia starts implementing Minsk agreements (Rappeport and MacFarquhar, 2017). Consequently, on 8 March 2018, the United States Department of the Treasury approved a new list of sanctions, adding to it the names of three more Russian individuals and nine entities.

Russians expansion in to Ukraine, annexation of Crimea and the increasing military cooperation with African countries in an emerging menace for Europe and the West. As such, the EU adopted in July 2014 and strengthened in September 2018, economic sanctions targeting Russian financial, defence and energy sectors. They restricted Russian access to EU capital markets, including nationals and companies overseas, and placing arms embargo, and a ban on exports of innovative extractive technology.

EU Sanctions against Russia under Global Programmes

The present situation which some scholars link to the 1919 Paris Peace Conference, as tabling sanctions, while the 'game' is still on. EU sanctions are drawn from the EU's Common Foreign and Security Policy, and as such belong to a wider framework when dealing with non-EU countries. In as much as, the sanctions aim to achieve policy change to country's which constitute a menace by promoting the values and principles inscribed within the Common Foreign and Security

Policy, while at the same time they target governments or non-EU countries, entities (companies), terrorist groups or jihadists and militias (Council of the European Union 2019). With increasing aggressor and terrorism in the region, the EU's Common and Foreign Security Policy, the EU has put in place 42 sanctions programmes, leading the second place, after US (first) of restrictive measures, in the world (Russell, 2018b: 1).

The EU was resolute in imposing sanctions on Russia after what was considered to be an illegal annexation of Crimea and destabilisation of Ukraine, which included the breaching of the country's territorial integrity. In light of this, the EU implemented several restrictive measures (EU Delegation to the Russian Federation, 2018):

a) diplomatic measures;

b) individual restrictive measures (asset freeze and travel restrictions);

c) restrictions on economic relations with Crimea and Sevastopol;

d) economic sanctions; and

e) restrictions on economic cooperation. Apropos the diplomatic measures, following the annexation of Crimea, the EU decided not to go with the organisation of the EU-Russia and G8 summits that were scheduled for Sochi (the G7 was instead organised in Brussels).

Furthermore, the EU Member States halted the negotiations on Russia's membership in the Organisation for Economic Co-operation and Development and the International Energy Agency. When it comes to individual restrictive measures, assets were frozen, and travel ban restrictions enforced for 155 people and 44 entities suspected of undertaking activities leading to the breach of international law, sovereignty and independence. Example of those implicated were: Sergey Valeryevich Aksyonov, Prime Minister of Crimea, Vladimir Denis Valentinovich Berezovskiy, commander of the Ukrainian Navy, Leonid Eduardovich Slutski, Commonwealth of Independent States (CIS) Chairman, and many others (Council Decision 2014/145/CFSP). Companies such as the Sevastopol and Kerch Commercial Seaport companies (European Parliament, 2016) also felt under the sanctions.

Last but not least, measures concerning economic cooperation were adopted in July 2014 and entailed the following: annulment of future financing operations in Russia by the European Investment Bank (EIB); agreement by EU member states on a common stance with respect to the coordination of their positions within the European Bank for Reconstruction and Development's (EBRD) financing of new operations in the Russian Federation; review of some of the EU bilateral and regional cooperation programmes with Russia, and complete annulment of others (Schellinck, 2018).

During the European Council's summit in Brussels on 13 December 2018, the EU leaders unanimously agreed to prolong economic sanctions against Russia for meddling in another country's internal affairs. Additionally, EU leaders condemned the most recent confrontation between Russia and Ukraine, when Russia seized three Ukrainian ships that were sailing off the coast of Crimea under the pretext that they illegally entered its territorial waters.

President Putin spoke of Ukrainian president Petro Poroshenko's intentions to deliberately provoke confrontation in the Kerch Strait for the sake of boosting his own popularity in the lead-up to the presidential elections in March 2019

(Sheftalovich, 2018). The European Council, on the other hand, requested "immediate release of all detained Ukrainian seamen as well as the return of the seized vessels and free passage of all ships through the Kerch Straits." In addition, EU leaders reconfirmed their "commitment to international law, the sovereignty, territorial integrity and independence of Ukraine and the EU's policy of non-recognition of the illegal annexation of Crimea" (European Council, 2018: 3).

In this respect, the sanctions imposed in 2014 were only the beginning of a series of sanctions that are to be renewed in years to come. On top of the Ukraine-related sanctions, since 2018, the EU has adopted three global sanctions programmes, on chemical weapons, cyber-attacks and human rights abuses. These impose visa bans, asset freezes and financial restrictions on individuals and entities from all over the world. Although global in scope, all three were largely inspired by Russian activities, and many of the names on the lists are from Russia.

Chemical Weapons

On 15 October 2018, the EU adopted sanctions against individuals and organisations involved in manufacturing and using chemical weapons, as defined by the Chemical Weapons Convention. Ten out of the 15 individuals on the list are Russians (while the others, were Syrians). The two agents who carried out the attempted assassination in 2018 of Sergey Skripal and two of their superiors from Russian military intelligence were among the first to be added to the list, in January 2019. After the Skripal incident, 18 EU Member States expelled 35 Russian diplomats. A further six senior officials from the presidential administration, government and Federal Security Service were added in October 2020, following a second attack on Alexey Navalny in August 2020.

Cyber-attack sanctions

Adopted on 17 May 2020, these concern individuals and organisations involved in cyber-attacks representing a significant threat to the EU and its Member States[20]. All of the six Russian individuals on the list (the remaining two designees are from China) are from the GRU (Main Intelligence Directorate) military intelligence service. Four agents were listed for an attempted hack of the Organisation for the Prohibition of Chemical Weapons in April 2018, while a further two were involved in an April 2015 cyber-attack on the German Bundestag.

Human rights sanctions

For many years, the EU raised concerns about human rights abuses in Russia, but had no legal instrument to adopt sanctions against those responsible. Finally, in December 2020, the EU adopted a global human rights sanctions regime, partly modelled on the U.S. Global Magnitsky Act of 2016. Again, Russians feature prominently on the list (six out of 15 names); four of them, from law enforcement, security and prisons services, are sanctioned for their role in the arrest, sentencing and imprisonment of opposition activist Alexey Navalny, as well as in repression of the resulting protests (January-February 2021); the remaining two are senior Chechen figures implicated in persecution of LGBT persons since 2017 (Chechen leader Ramzan Kadyrov was already designated in 2014 by Ukraine-related sanctions)[21].

---

20 https://www.readkong.com/page/sanctions-and-do-they-work-in-depth-analysis-european-1495755

21 https://www.readkong.com/page/sanctions-and-do-they-work-in-depth-analysis-european-1495755

President Putin: a threat to Biden's administration

"None of us should be fooled. None of us will be fooled. There is no justification." According to Biden, Russian forces rolled into rebel-held areas in eastern Ukraine and Putin's recognition of the independence of the separatist regions in defiance of U.S. and European pose a strategic menace to repositioning of additional U.S. troops to the Baltic nations on NATO's eastern flank bordering Russia.

Biden, though, did hold back some of the broadest and toughest of the financial penalties contemplated by the U.S., including sanctions that would reinforce the hold that Germany put on any startup of the Nord Stream 2 pipeline; an export ban that would deny Russia U.S. high tech for its industries and military; and sweeping bans that could cripple Russia's ability to do business with the rest of the world.

Biden said he was moving additional U.S. troops to the Baltics, though he described the deployments as purely "defensive," asserting, "We have no intention of fighting Russia."[22] The U.S. is sending about 800 infantry troops and 40 attack aircraft to NATO's eastern flank from other locations within Europe, according to a senior defence official. In addition, a contingent of F-35 strike fighters and AH-64 Apache attack helicopters will also be relocated[23].

Putin said the crisis could be resolved if Kyiv recognizes Russia's sovereignty over Crimea, the Black Sea peninsula that Moscow annexed after seizing it from Ukraine in 2014, renounces its bid to join NATO and partially demilitarizes[24].

---

22 https://www.kold.com/2022/02/22/russia-flexes-military-ukraine-move-west-respond//

23 https://ktla.com/news/nationworld/western-leaders-allege-russian-troops-have-moved-into-east-ukraine/

24 https://apnews.com/article/russia-ukraine-business-europe-russia-vladimir-putin-46cef648807d0e3c2bac9793ad9022a6

The West has decried the annexation of Crimea as a violation of international law and has previously flatly rejected permanently barring Ukraine from NATO[25].

If Putin pushes farther into Ukraine, NATO chief Jens Stoltenberg insisted the West would move in lockstep. "If Russia decides once again to use force against Ukraine, there will be even stronger sanctions, even a higher price to pay," he said. British Prime Minister Boris Johnson said the U.K. would slap sanctions on five Russian banks and three wealthy individuals[26]. He warned a full-scale offensive would bring "further powerful sanctions."[27]

Dialogue a necessity for international 'game' in Ukraine

If peace talks fail, the Russian military has several options to advance into Ukraine through northern, central, and southern invasion routes[28]. But a Russian attempt to seize and hold territory will not necessarily be easy and will likely be impacted by challenges from weather, urban combat, command and control, logistics, and the morale of Russian troops and the Ukrainian population. The United States and its European allies and partners should be prepared for an invasion by taking immediate economic, diplomatic, military, intelligence, and humanitarian steps to aid Ukraine and its population and shore up defences along the North Atlantic Treaty Organization's (NATO) eastern flank.

With an ideological basis for action in place, the next step is to create a casus belli—justification for war consistent

---

25 https://www.wect.com/2022/02/22/russia-flexes-military-ukraine-move-west-respond//

26 https://www.wsj.com/articles/u-k-to-boost-defence-collaboration-with-india-11650638778

27 https://globalnews.ca/news/8637243/united-states-unveil-sanctions-russia-ukraine-conflict/

28 https://www.csis.org/analysis/russias-possible-invasion-ukraine/

with the Kremlin-manufactured image of Ukraine. Pretexts for an attack could range from a straightforward breakdown of security talks to a stage-managed incident similar to the provocations at Mukden, Gleiwitz, and Mainila that provided justification for Japan's invasion of Manchuria, Germany's invasion of Poland, and the Soviet Union's attack on Finland, respectively[29]. This is why the bizarre claim of Defence Minister Sergey Shoigu posted on the Kremlin's official website of American mercenaries preparing a "provocation" with chemical weapons in Ukraine is ominous and might foreshadow just the type of "incident" the Kremlin would prepare.

Once there is a casus belli, cyberattacks will likely follow to degrade Ukraine's military command and control systems and public communications and electrical grids. Next, kinetic operations will likely begin with air and missile strikes against Ukraine's air force and air defence systems. Once air superiority is established, Russian ground forces would move forward, slightly preceded by special operations to degrade further command and control capabilities and delay the mobilization of reserves by conducting bombings, assassinations, and sabotage operations.

Impacts of Sanctions on Russian Economy

With the decision to prolong the sanctions initially imposed on Russia in 2014, both the U.S. and EU are determined to pursue foreign policy objectives that were defined following the annexation of Crimea. The unanimous decision to prolong the sanctions by the European Council in December 2018, speaks to the EU's unity on the sanctions, regardless of the status quo and failure to improve the situation on the ground in Ukraine. The U.S. pro-Ukrainian foreign policy also speaks in favour of supporting the territorial integrity

---

29 https://bilgi90.com/post/why-is-russia-invading-ukraine.p113648

of Ukraine and insistence on condemnation of Russia's sanctions.

The impact of sanctions on Russia can be assessed in various ways. From a political standpoint, the sanctions failed to politically isolate Russia and make the country refrain from striking deals with other major world powers. Following the introduction of sanctions by the West, Russia turned to the East, mainly to China, which is seen as an increasingly important partner. In economic terms, China is in a position to project regional and global power and influence (Ikenberry, 2014: 51). This subsequently leads the Russian foreign policy towards the East with the hope of setting the groundwork for curtailing U.S. supremacy in the global sphere. China, on the other hand, welcomes the possibility of diminishing U.S. influence in the Asia-Pacific.

The possibilities for Sino-Russian cooperation mostly boil down to arms trade and technology transfer, with energy cooperation developing at a moderate pace. A series of economic reforms that started in China more than four decades ago laid the foundation for expanding China's political and economic influence internationally and for catching up with the U.S. in economic terms (Carlsson et al., 2015: 4). Although rapprochement between Russia and China is nothing new, starting from 2014 the cooperation has intensified, mostly through the China-initiated Silk Road Economic Belt and the Eurasian Economic Union led by Russia. Sino-Russian strategic alignment was proven also in the case of Crimea when China refused to criticize Moscow and abstained from the UN Security Council's resolution on the Crimea referendum.

Regarding the economic impact of sanctions, Russia's economy suffered a sharp decline in mid-2014, following the Crimean matter and the crisis in Ukraine, thus implying that the reasons for such a downturn could be found in the imposition of the sanctions. However, the ensuing recession cannot be entirely blamed on sanctions as Russia's economic performance has always been closely correlated with crude oil prices, due to its reliance on fossil fuels, which generate 70 % of its export earnings (Russell, 2018: 7). Regardless, the energy sector is a direct target of sanctions, which forced international oil companies, such as Shell and Exxon Mobile, to suspend their project plans with Gazpromneft, thereby stripping the Russian oil magnum of opportunities for sharing technology and skills with their Western counterparts and implying that up to $500bn in planned investment was forsaken (Gould-Davies, 2018: 11).

Foreign bank exposure and FDI inflows have halved since 2013, whereas the proportion of Russian interbank loans and deposits outside the country declined from 60% to 37%. In just the first three years of sanctions, the ruble's average annual exchange rate in 2014-2016 against the euro depreciated by over 40% and by over 50% against the U.S. dollar (Korhonen et al. 2018: 11). In 2014, foreign liabilities in the private sector decreased by $37 billion in comparison to 2013, when an increase of $115 billion was observed (Gurvich and Prilepskiy, 2015: 360-361).

Given that, even during the Cold War, the Soviet Union imported technology from the West (the U.S. and Europe), it is highly likely that Russia will not be able to compensate for its declining production in traditional fields. Therefore, these sanctions might have a much larger impact in the long run since no suitable substitutes for acquiring new technology have so far been found elsewhere (Korhonen et al. 2018: 13). What is more, the U.S. sanctions that restricted Russian access to global financial markets and the acquisition of equipment for new energy projects will have an even greater effect in the long run, especially if the U.S. bans loans to the

Russian government in the near future. All these measures, understood by investors as a negative signal, were followed by a significant outflow of private capital from Russia (Tyll et al.2018: 26).

The sanctions have also had an impact on EU-Russia trade relations, with trade continuously decreasing since 2012, dropping by 44% between 2012 and 2016 from €339 billion in 2012 to €191 billion in 2016 (European Commission, 2019). Particular Member States also had much to lose in terms of exports to Russia throughout the sanctions period. Germany accounts for more than 40% of Western losses, affected by the sanctions, as the largest importer from Russia in the EU with €32 857 million and the highest share in total extra-EU imports.

However, Germany was also the country to suffer the most, through its €6 871 million trade deficit with Russia. Besides Germany, Italy and France also had to deal with high export losses during the period of sanctions. In terms of weakening EU exports, in 2016 alone, France experienced a decline of €1630 million in value added and 23,000 jobs being endangered due to the sanctions (European Parliament 2017: 12). On the other hand, in the agri-food sector, Italy suffered losses amounting to €850 million due to the loss in exports and more than €10 billion on the export of Italian-made produce (European Parliament 2017b). Nonetheless, despite the decline in trade during some years of sanctions, countries continued to sustain their relationship with Russia by concluding bilateral agreements and deepening their economic and political exchanges. On 4 July 2019, during his visit to Moscow, Italian Prime Minister Conte emphasized on the "excellent relations countries enjoy" and highlighted the growth in trade in 2018, which increased "by almost 13% to $27 billion" (Kremlin, 2019).

Economic sanctions are typically coercive policy instruments that seek to alter another country's behaviour by targeting its economic welfare. Despite being one of the most frequently deployed foreign policy tools, scholars contend that economic sanctions rarely achieve their objectives. The most comprehensive sanctions on Russia were imposed in 2014, following the annexation of Crimea and the violent unrests that erupted in eastern Ukraine. Not only did the events lead to another setback in relations between Russia and the West but they also resulted in the unanimous imposition of sanctions by Western powers. Drawing on the theory of international economic sanctions, this paper sought to examine the nature of the sanctions on Russia, their application and impact.

The decision to impose measures on Russia arose from the unanimous decision that the Russian Federation breached international law by annexing Crimea and violating the territorial sovereignty of Ukraine. Following the annexation of Crimea and the unrests in eastern Ukraine, the sanctions that were initially deployed included a limited number of travel restrictions, restrictions on economic cooperation and asset freezes, which specifically targeted certain individuals and companies in the Crimean Peninsula.

The groups, individuals, and companies that were targeted for inclusion on the list were all under suspicion of undermining democratic processes in the Ukraine, thus presenting a threat to the peace, security, integrity and stability of Ukraine (Korhonen, 2018: 4-5). Although the EU and the U.S. were closely aligned on the imposition of the sanctions in 2014, several differences could be spotted in their approaches. Unlike the EU, the sanctions imposed by the U.S. are open-ended and remain in force until a decision is taken to lift them and are broader in scope than those implemented by the EU (Russell, 2018b: 3). While the EU sanctions included, among others, diplomatic measures, asset freezes and travel restrictions, and bans on the importation of goods from Crimea and Sevastopol, the U.S. imposed sanctions targeting and blocking specific individuals and entities, and targeting determined sectors of the Russian economy, banning transactions such as oil exports, exploration technology, and implementing measures banning trade to and from Crimea and investment in the region (Smith, 2018: 5).

The immediate effect of sanctions on the Russian economy could not be readily seen due to other factors such as the decline of the ruble and the fact that the performance of the Russian economy correlates with the price of crude oil. The Russian public sector depends heavily on the national economy and price fluctuation in the oil and gas industry, which requires the federal government to promptly discharge its expenditure obligations (Sabitova and Shavaleyeva, 2015: 427). However, financial sanctions have had an indirect effect on the Russian economy in terms of the decreasing foreign direct investment, fewer borrowing opportunities for companies and banks not directly targeted by the sanctions, and lower capital inflow into the government debt market (Gurvich and Prilepskiy, 2015: 384).

The Russian energy sector suffered financial losses due to international oil companies suspending their project plans with Gazpromneft, consequently depriving Russia of knowledge and technology sharing processes. These sanctions have also had an influence on EU-Russia trade relations to a substantial extent, with the trade ratio dropping by 44% between 2012 and 2016. Reports revealed that the sanctions affected not only the Russian economy but also EU Member States, which traditionally nurture good trade relations with Moscow. Germany has suffered most with the trade deficit standing at €6 871 million, whereas Italy and France experienced the highest losses in export throughout the sanctions regime.

In his recent work entitled "The Technology of Victory," Igor Panarin, a leading advocate for Russian information warfare, boasted about the nearly flawless Russian operation to seize and annex Crimea. He celebrated the campaign's success in avoiding armed violence and preempting American interference. While pointing to neoconservative ideals of justice, spirituality, and "true" liberty, he praised the use of blackmail, intimidation, and deception in the face of international dithering in the West. He attributed the success to the personal leadership and direct control of Vladimir Putin.

Conclusion

On March 21, Putin signed the annexation of Crimea into Russian law. The seizure of all Ukrainian military installations on the peninsula concluded over the next two days as Russian forces massed along Ukraine's northeastern border. Finally, the last Ukrainian military personnel were ordered off the peninsula on March 24.

On March 31, soon after a brief removal of some Russian forces from the border region of Rostov at the urging of the United States, Russia initiated the invasion of the Donbass region of eastern Ukraine. However, the annexation and removal of Ukrainian forces was not the end of the Crimea crisis. As recounted in the analysis below, there followed a series of nuclear posturing and threats explicitly concerning Crimea, and, despite being concurrent with the invasion of Donbass, the crisis in Crimea was treated as separate from that in Donbass in high-level negotiations. Resolution of the crisis, then, is best dated as June 1, 2015, after which nuclear posturing and threats around Crimea appeared to cease[30].

---

30 https://www.jhuapl.edu/Content/documents/RussianInvasionCrimeanPen-
    insula.pdf

Russia's objective was to secure the Crimean Peninsula in order to ensure strategic access, allegedly to protect Russian-speaking populations and to prevent integration of Ukraine into NATO. Russia succeeded in securing de facto control of Crimea and ostensibly succeeded in insulating Russian-speaking residents of Crimea from alleged Ukrainian nationalist reprisals. The prospect of Ukrainian integration into NATO also did not materialize in the years since the crisis. While there were indications that Russian actions in Donbass alongside the crisis in Crimea sought to connect separatist regions in eastern Ukraine to the peninsula as a new region ("Novorossiya"), this analysis does not consider that effort to be an objective of the initial invasion of Crimea, which was responsive to the removal of Viktor Yanukovych[31]. In summary, Russia emerged from the crisis in Crimea as the victor.

Ukraine, the EU, and the United States, on the other hand, once faced with the invasion of Crimea, sought to de-escalate tensions and avoid an armed conflict while ensuring the territorial integrity of Ukraine through negotiations and sanctions. The negotiations and sanctions failed to maintain Ukraine's territorial integrity or de-escalate the crisis—Russia secured de facto military and administrative control of Ukraine's Crimean Peninsula, and armed conflict would nevertheless come to be imposed on Ukraine in Donbass.

Reading Nick Wadhams narrative on the present U.S. administration in Bloomberg News. he pointed out that; Biden's Own Aides Feared His Sanctions Wouldn't Stop Putin with no alternatives, a 'tired' foreign policy tool now faces a high-stakes test on the Russia-Ukraine border. More than a dozen current and former U.S. officials, many of

---

31 https://politicalwire.com/2022/02/24/biden-aides-feared-sanctions-strategy-wouldnt-work/

whom helped assemble the response, told Bloomberg News they've been deeply dubious that sanctions would change Putin's behavior. Yet after Biden made clear last year that the U.S. would not send troops or heavy weapons to Ukraine, there were no other solid options[32]. It was left to his team to try to prove, for the first time, that the threat of economic warfare against a major adversary like Russia would suffice when military deterrence wasn't an option.

As U.S. leaders grew wary of repeating military debacles in Iraq and Afghanistan, the relative ease of imposing economic sanctions has made them the foreign-policy option of first resort, despite a growing body of evidence that they often fail to achieve their goals. In some cases, experience has shown that sanctions only entrench undesirable behavior from the parties they target. Those limitations are compounded by the prospect that the toughest sanctions on Russia — those that might actually alter Putin's behavior — would also imperil the U.S. and global economies, already beset by surging prices for oil and other commodities.

Biden's team — some of whom had criticized Trump and his predecessors for using sanctions too often and without plans for lifting them — ultimately adopted a strategy with sanctions at its center. "The tool of sanctions has become a tired tool," said Stephen Biegun, the former deputy secretary of state under Donald Trump and a veteran of other Republican administrations, who helped formulate U.S. policy toward North Korea. Biegun said Biden's administration has no good options for countering Putin, but the use of sanctions "has not seemed to significantly alter the behavior of any foreign party whose actions are of concern to the United States."[33]

---

32 https://politicalwire.com/2022/02/24/biden-aides-feared-sanctions-strategy-wouldnt-work/

33 https://fortune.com/2022/02/24/biden-aides-doubt-russia-sanctions-plan-change-putin-behavior-ukraine/

Some top banks would face additional restrictions, such as asset freezes. The U.S. has also warned of imposing limits on the sale of goods with complex American technology such as microchips, an attack that would hit Russia's aviation and oil sectors as well as its military.

Putin has been more blunt. "To hell with those sanctions," he told Itar-Tass in 2020. "It made us use our brains."[34] "The Russian economy has largely adjusted to those sanctions," said Andrea Kendall-Taylor, a senior fellow at the Center for a New American Security[35]. "They have pursued a very significant export substitution policy in other parts of the Russian economy that are now booming." One example: Russia's agriculture sector, including meat and cheese production, is booming[36].

---

34 https://fortune.com/2022/02/24/biden-aides-doubt-russia-sanctions-plan-change-putin-behavior-ukraine/amp//

35 https://www.cnas.org/press/in-the-news/bidens-own-aides-feared-his-sanc-tions-wouldnt-stop-putin

36 ibid

Bibliography

Aid, Mathew. "More on Russian Spetsnaz Operations in Crimea and along Ukrainian Border." Personal blog, April 10, 2014, http://www.matthewaid.com/post/82280374358/more-on-russian-spetsnaz-operations-incrimea-and.

———. "The Role of the GRU in Russia's Takeover of the Crimea." Personal blog, March 26, 2014, http://www.matthewaid.com/post/80776580075/the-role-of-the-gru-in-russias-takeover-of-the.

Balouziyeh, John. "Russia's Annexation of Crimea: An Analysis Under the Principles of Jus Ad Bellum." LexisNexisInternational Law (blog), April 14, 2014. http://www.lexisnexis.com/legalnewsroom/international-law/b/international-law-blog/archive/2014/04/14/russia-s-annexation-of-crimea-an-analysis-under-the-principles-ofjus-ad-bellum.aspx.

Batyuk, Vladimir. "The End of the Cold War: A Russian View." History Today 49, no. 4 (1999): http://www.historytoday.com/vladimir-batyuk/end-cold-war-russian-view.

Bauman, Robert F. Russian-Soviet Unconventional Wars in the Caucasus, Central Asia, and Afghanistan.

Leavenworth Papers vol. 20. Fort Leavenworth, KS: Combat Studies Institute, U.S. Army Command and General Staff College, 1993.

Berzins, Janis. Russia's New Generation Warfare in Ukraine: Implications for Latvian Defence Policy. Riga: National Defence Academy of Latvia, 2014.

Boltenkov, Dmitry, Aleksey Gayday, Anton Karnaukhov, Anton Lavrov, and Vyacheslav Tseluiko. Russia's New Army. Edited by Mikhail Barabanov. Moscow: Centre for Analysis of Strategies and Technologies, 2011.

Bugriy, Maksym. "The Crimean Operation: Russian Force and Tactics," Eurasia Daily Monitor 11 no. 61 (April 1, 2014): http://www.jamestown.org/ regions/europe/single/?tx_ttnews[pointer]=6&tx_ttnews[tt_news]=42164&tx_ttnews[backPid]=51&cHash=fc393270652afcca3fe0563fcc63c5a0#. VT5gQpOjYgk.

Center for Strategic and International Studies. "The Ukraine Crisis Timeline." 2014. http://csis.org/ukraine/index.htm.

Charbonneau, Louis. "U.N. Says Pro-Russia Rebels in Ukraine Murder, Kidnap, and Torture." Reuters,August 26, 2014, http://www.reuters.com/article/2014/08/26/us-ukraine-crisis-rights-unidUSKBN0gq1TA20140826.

Coffey, Michael. "Military Learning between the Chechen Wars." Vestnik (Journal of Russian and Asian Studies), no. 5(Fall 2006): http://www.sras.org/military_learning_between_the-chechen_wars.

Darczewska, Jolanta. "The Anatomy of Russian Information Warfare: The Crimean Operation, A Case Study." Point ofView vol. 42. Warsaw: Center for Eastern Studies, 2014.

Englund, Will. "In Ukraine, Death and Protest Come with a History." Washington Post, January 28, 2014, http://www.washingtonpost.com/world/europe/in-ukraine-death-and-protest-come-with-a-history/2014/01/28/087daa72-85ca-11e3-8742-668814928ae4_story.html.

Frye, Barbara, Ioana Caloianu, and Anders Ryehauge. "Ukrainian Troops Close in on Rebel Stronghold, Armenian Villager Dies in Azerbaijan Custody." Transitions Online, August 11, 2014.

Gerasimov, Valery. "The Value of Science in Prediction." Military-Industrial Kurier, February 27, 2013.

German, Tracey. Russia and the Caspian Sea: Projecting Power or Competing for Influence? Carlisle, PA: U.S. Army War College, 2014.

glhermine. "Ukraine 2012." World Elections (blog), January 19, 2010, https://welections.wordpress.com/2010/01/19/ukraine-2010/.

Gowan, Richard. "West Needs New Rules to Contain Proxy Wars with Russia." World Politics Review, July 21, 2014.

Gudelis, Mykolas. "Rethinking the People's Revolution: The Role of the Soviet Union and National Elites in Lithuania's

Velvet Revolution." Canon (Interdisciplinary Journal of the New School for Social Research) (Winter 2011): http://canononline.org/?s=Rethinking+the+People%E2%80%99s+Revolution.

Gvosdev, Nikolas K. "Ukraine's Ancient Hatreds." National Interest, no. 132 (July–August 2014).

Herd, Graeme P., and Ella Akerman. "Russian Strategic Realignment and the Post-Post-Cold War Era?"Security Dialogue 33, no. 3 (2002): 357–372.

Herspring, Dale R., and Roger N. McDermott. "Serdyukov Promotes Systemic Russian Military Reform." Orbis 54,no. 2 (2010): 284–301.

Hirst, Tomas. "Meet the 'Pocket Army' Funded by Sacked Ukrainian Billionaire Igor Kolomoisky." Business Insider, March 28, 2015, http://www.businessinsider.com/meet-the-pocket-army-funded-by-sacked-ukrainianbillionaire-igor-kolomoisky-2015-3.

Humphries, Richard. "Transnistria: Relic of a Bygone Era." Japan Times, October 8, 2001.

Huntington, Samuel P. (ed.). The Clash of Civilizations?: The Debate. Tampa, FL: Foreign Affairs, 1993. http://www.foreignaffairs.com/articles/48950/samuel-p-huntington/the-clash-of-civilizations.

Ignatius, David. "Russia's Military Delivers a Striking Lesson in Crimea." Washington Post, March 18, 2014, http://www.washingtonpost.com/opinions/david-ignatius-russias-military-delivers-a-striking-lesson-incrimea/2014/03/18/c1273044-aed7-11e3-9627-c65021d6d572_story.html.

Interfax-Ukraine. "Tymoshenko: 'Resistance Movement' in Ukraine Has over 20,000 Members." KyivPost, May 16, 2014, http://www.kyivpost.com/content/ukraine/tymoshenko-resistance-movement-in-ukraine-hasover-20000-members-348207.html.

Karatnycky, Adrian. "Ukraine's Orange Revolution." Foreign Affairs, March/April 2005.

King, Charles. "The Five-Day War: Managing Moscow After the Georgia Crisis." Foreign Affairs, November/ December 2008.

Kmakhidze, Irakliy. "Armed Forces of Russian Federation Spotted along the Ukrainian Border and in Donbas."Euromaidan Press, August 27, 2014, http://euromaidanpress.com/2014/08/27/armed-forces-of-russianfederation-spotted-along-the-ukrainian-border-and-in-donbas/.

Kozlov, Sergi. "FSB Special Forces: 1998-2010." Argentura, September 8, 2010, http://www.argentura.ru/english/spetsnaz/FSBspecialforces/.

Kramer, Mark. "The Soviet Union, the Warsaw Pact, and the Polish Crisis of 1980-81." In The Solidarity Movement

and Perspectives on the Last Decade of the Cold War, edited by Lee Trepanier et al. Krakow: AFM Publishing House, 2010.

Maigre, Merle, "Crimea—The Achilles Heel of Ukraine." International Centre for Defence Studies, 2008.

Meadows, David. "Understanding Russia's Proxy War in Eastern Ukraine." Security Sector Reform Resource Centre, August 12, 2014, http://www.ssrresourcecentre.org/2014/08/12/understanding-russias-proxy-war-in-easternukraine/.

Meyer, Karl E., and Shareen B. Brysac. Tournament of Shadows: The Great Game and the Race for Empire in Central Asia. New York: Basic Books, 1999.

Niblett, Robin. "Nato Must Focus on the 'Hybrid Wars' Being Waged on the West." Financial Times, July 17, 2014.

Olearchyk, Roman, and Neil Buckley. "How Russia Forced Ukraine into A Ceasefire with Rebels." Financial Times,September 12, 2014.

"Oligarchs as Nation's Saviors? Berezovsky Justifies Himself." St. Petersburg Times, October 20, 2000.

Pagani, Pierluigi. "Crimea—The Russian Cyber Strategy to Hit Ukraine." InfoSec Institute, March 11, 2014, http://resources. infosecinstitute.com/crimea-russian-cyber-strategy-hit-ukraine/.

Powell, Bill. "How the KGB (and Friends) Took Over Russia's Economy." Fortune, September 4, 2008.

"Russia Defence & Security Report." Russia Defence & Security Report, no. 3 07/01 (2014).

Safire, William. "Siloviki Versus Oligarchy." New York Times, November 5, 2003.

Sarotte, Mary E. "A Broken Promise? What the West Really Told Moscow about NATO Expansion." Foreign Affairs,September–October 2014.

Saytas, Andrius, and Aija Krutaine. "Ukraine Crisis Stokes Baltic Nerves Over Russia." Reuters, March 3, 2014.

Schenkkan, Nate. "Band of Outsiders: How Sanctions Will Strengthen Putin's Regional Clout." Foreign Affairs, September–October 2014.

Sharafutdinova, Gulnaz. Political Consequences of Crony Capitalism Inside Russia. Contemporary European Politicsand Society. Notre Dame, IN: University of Notre Dame Press, 2010.

Shuster, Simon. "Meet the Cossack 'Wolves' Doing Russia's Dirty Work in Ukraine." Time, May 2014.

Sindelar, Daisy. "In Eastern Ukraine, The Hunt for A Smoking Gun—And a Real Russian Holding It." Radio Free Europe/ Radio Liberty, April 15, 2014, http://www.rferl.org/content/ ukraine-smoking-russian-gun/25334376.html.

Thompson, Mark. "Sanctions Hit Russian Oil and Banks." CNN Money, September 12, 2014.

"The Ukraine Crisis Timeline." Center for Strategic and International Studies 2014. http://csis.org/ukraine/index. htm.

U.S. Central Intelligence Agency. "Ukraine." The World Factbook. https://www.cia.gov/library/publications/the-worldfactbook/geos/up.html.

Weaver, Courtney. "Malofeev: The Russian Billionaire Linking Moscow to the Rebels." Financial Times, July 24, 2014.

Agreement on the Settlement of Crisis in Ukraine. Kyiv, 21 February 2014. Retrieved from: http:// www.auswaertiges amt.de/cae/ servlet/contentblob/671350/publicationFile/190027/140221- UKR_Erklaerung.pdf

100% sure Berkut police didn't shoot people in Kyiv' – ex-Ukrainian interior minister. (2014, April 5) RT. Retrieved from: https:// www.rt.com/news/snipers-ukrainemaidan-berkut-613/

Amnesty International (2015) The Amnesty International Report 2014- 2015. Ukraine Report. Retrieved from: https://www. amnesty.org/en/countries/europe-and-central-asia/ukraine/ report-ukraine/

Dougherty, J & Pfaltzgraff, R. (1981) Contending Theories of International Relations. A Comprehensive Survey. New York: Harper & Row, Publishers, Inc.

Joint Chiefs of Staff (2010) Department of Defence Dictionary of Military and Associated Terms. (Amendedversion Oct. 2015). [Ebray version].Retrieved from: http://www.dtic.mil/doctrine/dod_dictionary/

Lund, M. S. (2009) Conflict Prevention: Theory in Pursuit of Policy and Practice. In J. Bercovitch, V. Kremenyuk, W. Zartman (Eds.), The Sage Handbook Of Conflict Resolution (pp. 287-321). London: SAGE Publications Ltd.

Martínez de Murguía, B. (1999) Mediación y resolución de conflictos. Mexico City: Paidós. Moscow respects will expressed by population of Donetsk and Luhansk regions of Ukraine. (2014, May 12) Tas. Retrieved from: http://tass.ru/en/world/731214

Russia's Vladimir Putin 'to respect'Ukraine vote. (2014, May 23). BBC News. Retrieved from: http://w w w. b b c . c o m / n e w s / w o r l d -europe-27542057

Smith, A. (2014_b, April 22) Russia Hits Back at Biden: We Are Ready for 'Unfriendly Steps'. NBC News. Retrieved from: http://www.nbcnews.com/storyline/ukraine-crisis/russia-hits-backbiden-we-are-ready-unfriendlysteps-n86726

Ukraine crisis: Turchynov warns of'separatism' risk. (2014, February 25). BBC News. Retrieved from:http://www.bbc.com/news/worldeurope-26333587

AFP. "Ukraine Crisis Returns Specter of War, EU Chief Warns," Times of Israel, March 20, 2014. http://www.timesofisrael.com/ukraine-crisis-returns-specter-of-war-eu-chief-warns/.

Amos, Howard. "Ukraine Crisis Fuels Secession Calls in Pro-Russian South." Guardian, February 23, 2014.https://www.theguardian.com/world/2014/feb/23/ukraine-crisis-secession-russian-crimea.

AOWG (Asymmetric Operations Working Group). Ambiguous Threats and External Influences in the BalticStates and Poland, Phase 1: Understanding the Threat. Fort Meade, MD: Asymmetric Warfare Group,October 2014.

———. Ambiguous Threats and External Influences in the Baltic States and Poland, Phase 2: Assessing theThreat. Fort Meade, MD: Asymmetric Warfare Group, November 2015.

Arbman, Gunnar, and Charles Thornton. Russia's Tactical Nuclear Weapons. Part I: Background and PolicyIssues. FOI-R-1057-SE. Stockholm, Sweden: FOI—Swedish Defence Research Agency, November 2003.

"Are Nuclear Launchers in Crimea a Game-Changer?" Nukes of Hazard (blog). Center for ArmsControl and Non-Proliferation, May 18, 2015. https://armscontrolcenter.org/are-nuclear-launchersin-crimea-a-game-changer-2/.

"Armed Services Leaders Urge President to Act on Ukraine." Press release. House Armed ServicesCommittee, March 26, 2014, archived April 2, 2014. https://web.archive.org/web/20140402013349/

http://armedservices.house.gov/index.cfm/press-releases?ContentRecord_id=AE52EEAE-20D7-4C07-AE4B-1520D8287DD2.

Ashton, Catherine. "Statement by EU High Representative Catherine Ashton on the Developmentsin Ukraine's Crimea." European Union, 140301/01, March 1, 2014. https://web.archive.org/

web/20140319171915/http://eeas.europa.eu/statements/docs/2014/140301_01_en.pdf.

Ball, Joshua. "Escalate to De-Escalate: Russia's Nuclear Deterrence Strategy." Global Security Review, updatedJune 10, 2019. https://globalsecurityreview.com/nuclear-de-escalation-russias-deterrence-strategy/.

Bender, Jeremy. "Russia: We Have the Right to Put Nuclear Weapons in Crimea." Business Insider, December16, 2014. https://www.businessinsider.com/russia-we-can-put-nuclear-weapons-in-crimea-2014-12.

Berls, Robert E., Jr., and Leon Ratz. Rising Nuclear Dangers: Assessing the Risk of Nuclear Use in theEuro-Atlantic Region. Washington, DC: Nuclear Threat Initiative, October, 2015. https://media.nti.org/pdfs/NTI_Rising_Nuclear_Dangers_Paper_FINAL.pdf.

Binns, Daniel. "Army Airport Seized Ahead of Crimca Votc," Metro Herald (Ireland), March 10, 2014, 6.https://issuu.com/metroherald/docs/metroire20140310.

Booth, William, and Will Englund. "Tensions Rise in Crimea Amid Finger-Pointing." Washington Post,March 4, 2014.38 THE JOHNS HOPKINS UNIVERSITY APPLIED PHYSICS LABORATORY

Brady, Erik. "USA Won't Send Presidential Delegation to Sochi Paralympics." USA Today, March 3, 2014. https://www.usatoday.com/story/sports/olympics/sochi/2014/03/03/united-states-official-delegationsochi-paralympics/5976875/.

Brecher, Michael, and Jonathan Wilkenfeld. A Study of Crisis. Ann Arbor, MI: University of Michigan Press, 2000.

Brecher, Michael, Jonathan Wilkenfeld, Kyle Beardsley, Patrick James, and David Quinn. "CrimeaDonbass." 2017. https://drive.google.com/file/d/1UZflH9LAKUnTg3V4CjJcmvVQQzrb6sr-/view.

———. International Crisis Behavior Data Codebook, Version 12. 2017. http://sites.duke.edu/icbdata/data-collections/.

Budapest Memorandums on Security Assurances, 1994. Council on Foreign Relations, publishedDecember 5, 1994, archived from the original on January 29, 2016. https://web.archive.org/

web/20160129213053/http://www.cfr.org/nonproliferation-arms-control-and-disarmament/budapest-memorandums-security-assurances-1994/p32484.

Budjeryn, Mariana. "Was Ukraine's Nuclear Disarmament a Blunder?" World Affairs 179, no. 2 (Summer 2016): 9–20. https://journals.sagepub.com/doi/pdf/10.1177/0043820016673777.

Castle, Stephen, and Michael R. Gordon. "U.S. Imposes Visa Ban on 20 Ukrainian Officials as FurtherSanctions Are Threatened." New York Times, February 19, 2014. https://www.nytimes.com/2014/02/20/world/europe/ukraine-reaction.html.

"Chernobyl Accident 1986." World Nuclear Association. June 2019. http://www.world-nuclear.org/info/Safety-and-Security/Safety-of-Plants/Chernobyl-Accident/.

Chu, Henry, and Sergei L. Loiko. "Ukraine Leaders Vow Not to Cede Land; Russia Tightens Grip onCrimea." Los Angeles Times, March 9, 2014. https://www.latimes.com/world/la-xpm-2014-mar-09-lafg-wn-crimea-ukraine-russia-20140309-story.html.

Clements, Matthew. "Russian Military Intervention in Ukraine Dependent on Significant Escalation of Violence in Crimea." Jane's Intelligence Weekly, February 27, 2014.

Congressional Budget Office. Cost Estimate: S. 2124 Support for the Sovereignty, Integrity, Democracy, and Economic Stability of Ukraine Act of 2014, As reported by the Senate Committee on Foreign Relations on March 12, 2014. Washington, DC: Congressional Budget Office. March 24, 2014, http://www.cbo.gov/sites/default/files/cbofiles/attachments/s2124_0.pdf.

Conley, Jerry. "Orange Revolution of Ukraine: 2004–2005." In Casebook on Insurgency and Revolutionary Warfare, Volume II: 1962–2009, edited by Chuck Crossett, 625–644. Fort Bragg, NC: U.S. Army Special Operations Command, 2012.

Coyle, James J. Russia's Border Wars and Frozen Conflicts. Cham, Switzerland: Palgrave Macmillan, 2018.

"Crimean Parliament Sacks Regional Government, Approves Referendum." RT, February 27, 2014. https://on.rt.com/3pmh9s.

Crom, Pierre, and Eva Cukier. War in Ukraine. Eindhoven, the Netherlands: Lecturis, 2017.The RuSSiAN iNvASioN of The CRimeAN PeNiNSulA, 2014–2015 39

D'Anieri, Paul. Ukraine and Russia: From Civilized Divorce to Uncivil War. Cambridge: Cambridge University Press, 2019.

"Death Toll up to 13,000 in Ukraine Conflict, Says UN Rights Office." RFE/RL. February 26, 2019. https://www.rferl.org/a/death-toll-up-to-13-000-in-ukraine-conflict-says-un-rights-office/29791647.html.

DeYoung, Karen. "Obama Speaks with Putin by Phone, Calls on Russia to Pull Forces Back to Crimea Bases." Washington Post, March 1, 2014. https://www.washingtonpost.com/world/national-security/us-and-allies-try-to-decide-on-response-to-ukraine-crisis/2014/03/01/463d1922-a174-11e3-b8d8-94577ff66b28_story.html.

"Don't Mess With Nuclear Russia, Putin Warns at Youth Camp." Moscow Times, August 29, 2014. https://themoscowtimes.com/news/dont-mess-with-nuclear-russia-putin-warns-at-youth-camp-38885.

Dorell, Oren. "Ukraine May Have to Go Nuclear, Says Kyiv Lawmaker." USA Today, March 10, 2014. https://www.usatoday.com/story/news/world/2014/03/10/ukraine-nuclear/6250815/.

Dunham, Will. "Kerry Condemns Russia's 'Incredible Act of Aggression' in Ukraine." Reuters, March 2, 2014.https://www.reuters.com/article/us-ukraine-crisis-usa-kerry/kerry-condemns-russias-incredibleact-of-aggression-in-ukraine-idUSBREA210DG20140302.

"Eased Russian Customs Rules to Save Ukraine $1.5 Bln in 2014, Says Minister." Interfax-Ukraine,December 18, 2013. https://en.interfax.com.ua/news/economic/182691.html.

Editor. "Ukraine Liveblog: Day 7—Decoding Documents & Indicting Dictators." Interpreter, February24, 2014. http://www.interpretermag.com/ukraine-liveblog-day-7-decoding-documents-indictingdictators/#2308.

"The Effects of Armenia's Decision to Join the Customs Union." Stratfor, September 5, 2013. https://worldview.stratfor.com/article/effects-armenias-decision-join-customs-union.

"EP President Hopes Yanukovych Will Start Listening to Maidan Voices." Interfax-Ukraine, December 8,2013. http://en.interfax.com.ua/news/general/180163.html.

Erlanger, Steven. "Ukraine Rushes to Dampen Secessionist Mood in East; With Russia in Control of Crimea,Kyiv Worries that Region is Next to Fall." International New York Times, March 4, 2014.

"EU Diplomats Go to Demo Site in Kyiv." Interfax-Ukraine, December 9, 2013. http://en.interfax.com.ua/news/general/180376.html.

"EU Sanctions against Russia over Ukraine Crisis." European External Action Service. Accessed January 9,2020. Archived December 31, 2019. https://web.archive.org/web/20191231011325/https://europa.eu/newsroom/highlights/special-coverage/eu-sanctions-against-russia-over-ukraine-crisis_en.

"EuroMaidan Is the Largest Demonstration in EU History." UA Today, December 11, 2013. https://web.archive.org/web/20160304042135/http://old.uatoday.com/modules/myarticles/article_storyid_60689.html.

"EU's Füle Rues Ukraine's 'Missed Chance.' " Euronews, November 26, 2013. http://www.euronews.com/2013/11/26/eu-s-fulerues-ukraine-s-missed-chance.40 THE JOHNS HOPKINS UNIVERSITY APPLIED PHYSICS LABORATORY

Everett, Burgess, and Josh Gerstein. "Why Didn't the U.S. Know Sooner?" Politico, March 4, 2014, updatedMarch 5, 2014. https://www.politico.com/story/2014/03/united-states-barack-obama-ukraine-crimearussia-vladimir-putin-104264.

Felgenhauer, Pavel. "Kremlin Sees Ukraine Crisis as Part of Overall U.S.-Led Assault on Russia." Eurasia Daily Monitor 11, no. 159 (September 11, 2014). https://jamestown.org/program/kremlin-sees-ukrainecrisis-as-part-of-overall-us-led-assault-on-russia/.

———. "Putin Pushing Back against the West and Its Presumed Agents." Eurasia Daily Monitor 10,no. 223 (December 12, 2013). https://jamestown.org/program/putin-pushing-back-against-thewest-and-its-presumed-agents/.

———. "Putin: Ukraine Is a Battlefield for the New World Order." Eurasia Daily Monitor 11, no. 121 (July 3,2014). https://jamestown.org/program/putin-ukraine-is-a-battlefield-for-the-new-world-order/.

Frankel, Michael, James Scouras, and George Ullrich. Nonstrategic Nuclear Weapons at an Inflection Point.

National Security Perspective NSAD-R-17-024. Laurel, MD: Johns Hopkins University Applied Physics Laboratory, 2017.

Galleotti, Mark. Armies of Russia's War in Ukraine. Oxford, UK: Osprey Publishing, 2019.

Gardner, Hall. Crimea, Global Rivalry, and the Vengeance of History. New York: Palgrave Macmillan, 2015.

Goble, Paul. "Archives Show Stalin Was Ready to Give Hitler Ukraine and the Baltics." Euromaidan Press,June 20, 2016. http://euromaidanpress.com/2016/06/20/archives-show-stalin-was-ready-to-give-hitlerukraine-and-the-baltics-euromaidan-press/.

Goldberg, Jeffrey. "The Obama Doctrine." Atlantic, April 2016. https://www.theatlantic.com/magazine/archive/2016/04/the-obama-doctrine/471525/.

"Gorbachev Issues New Warning of Nuclear War over Ukraine." DW, January 9, 2015. https://p.dw.com/p/1EICZ.

Grant, Thomas D. Aggression against Ukraine: Territory, Responsibility, and International Law. New York:Palgrave Macmillan, 2015.

Greig, J. Michael, and Andrew J. Enterline. "National Material Capabilities (NMC) Data Documentation." Version 5.0. Correlates of War Project, February 1, 2017.

Grove, Thomas. "Russian Marine Kills Ukraine Navy Officer in Crimea, Says Ministry." Reuters, April 7,2017. https://www.reuters.com/article/us-ukraine-crisis-military/russian-marine-kills-ukraine-navyofficer-in-crimea-says-ministry-idUSBREA360GB20140407.

Guschin, Ivan. "U.S. Energy Department Suspends Peaceful Atom Projects with Russia." TASS, April 3, 2014. https://web.archive.org/web/20200109174440/https://tass.com/world/726421.

Herszenhorn, David M. "Crimea Votes to Secede From Ukraine as Russian Troops Keep Watch." NewYork Times, March 16, 2014. http://www.nytimes.com/2014/03/17/world/europe/crimea-ukrainesecession-vote-referendum.html?_r=0.The RuSSiAN iNvASioN of The CRimeAN PeNiNSulA, 2014–2015 41

Higgins, Andrew, and Steven Lee Myers. "As Putin Orders Drills in Crimea, Protesters' Clash Shows Region's Divide." New York Times, February 26, 2014. https://www.nytimes.com/2014/02/27/world/europe/russia.html.

Hoyle, Ben. "Putin Threat of Nuclear Showdown over Baltics; Putin Challenges Nato to Back off from Border." Times (UK), April 2, 2015. https://advance.lexis.com/api/document?co

llection=news&id=urn:contentItem:5FN8-JWM1-JBVM-Y2CM-00000-00&context=1516831.

Huzar, Bogdan. "Rosja przygotowuje się do zbrojnej interwencji na Ukrainie?" [Russia is preparing formilitary intervention in Ukraine?]. Newsweek, February 23, 2014, archived February 24, 2014. https://web.archive.org/web/20140224033624/http://blogi.newsweek.pl/Tekst/swiat/684527%2Crosja-przygotowuje-sie-do-zbrojnej-interwencji-na-ukrainie.html.

Interfax-Ukraine. "Rosselkhoznadzor: Russia Could Limit Food Imports from Ukraine." Kyiv Post, February 24, 2014. http://www.kyivpost.com/content/ukraine/rosselkhoznadzor-russia-could-limitfood-imports-from-ukraine-337529.html.

Jackson, David. "TV Anchor: Russia Can Turn U.S. 'into Radioactive Dust.' " USA Today, March 17, 2014. https://www.usatoday.com/story/theoval/2014/03/17/obama-russia-putin-ukraine-tv-anchorradioactive-dust/6515197.

Jivanda, Tomas. "Ukraine Crisis: Russia Carries out Massive Nuclear War Exercise Involving 10,000 Troops." Independent, March 30, 2014. http://www.independent.co.uk/news/world/europe/russia-carries-out-massive-nuclear-war-exercise-involving-10000-troops-9224290.html.

"Joint Statement of the NATO-Ukraine Commission." North Atlantic Treaty Organization. Press release (2015) 074, May 13, 2015. https://www.nato.int/cps/en/natohq/official_texts_119425.htm.

Kalb, Marvin. Imperial Gamble: Putin, Ukraine, and the New Cold War. Washington, DC: Brookings Institution Press, 2015.

Karmanau, Yuras, and Dalton Bennett. "Russia Reinforces Military Presence in Crimea." Associated Press, March 8, 2014, updated March 11, 2014. https://globalnews.ca/news/1195957/russian-troopsreported-on-the-move-again-in-crimea/.

Kashin, Vasiliy. "Khrushchev's Gift: The Questionable Ownership of Crimea." In Brothers Armed: Military Aspects of the Crisis in Ukraine, edited by Colby Howard and Ruslan Pukhov, 1–21. Minneapolis: East View Press, 2015.

Keck, Zachary. "Russia Threatens Nuclear Strikes over Crimea." Diplomat, July 11, 2014. https://thediplomat.com/2014/07/russia-threatens-nuclear-strikes-over-crimea/.

———. "Russia Threatens to Deploy Nuclear Weapons in Crimea." The Buzz (blog), National Interest, June 1, 2015. https://nationalinterest.org/blog/the-buzz/russia-threatens-deploy-nuclear-weapons-crimea-13013.

"Key MEPs Warn Ukraine Authorities Not to Use Force against Pro-Europe Protestors." Press release 20131126IPR26201. European Parliament, November 26, 2013. http://www.europarl.europa.eu/news/en/press-room/20131126IPR26201/key-meps-warn-ukraine-authorities-not-to-use-force-againstpro-europe-protestors.42 THE JOHNS HOPKINS UNIVERSITY APPLIED PHYSICS LABORATORY

Klymenko, Andrii. Human Rights Abuses in Russian-Occupied Crimea. Washington, DC: Atlantic Council and Freedom House, March 2015. https://freedomhouse.org/sites/default/files/2020-02/CrimeaReport_FINAL.pdf.

Kofman, Michael, Katya Migacheva, Brian Nichiporuk, Andrew Radin, Olesya Tkacheva, and Jenny Oberholtzer. Lessons from Russia's Operations in Crimea and Eastern Ukraine. Santa Monica, CA: RAND Corporation, 2017.

Koren, Marina. "The Ukraine Crisis Is Unsettling Decades-Old Nuclear-Weapons Agreements." National Journal, March 12, 2014. https://www.nationaljournal.com/s/60775.

Kristensen, Hans M. Non-Strategic Nuclear Weapons. Special Report No. 3. Washington, DC: Federation of American Scientists, May 2012. https://fas.org/_docs/Non_Strategic_Nuclear_Weapons.pdf.

———. "Nuclear Exercises Amidst Ukrainian Crisis: Time for Cooler Heads." Strategic Security (blog), Federation of American Scientists, May 16, 2014.https://fas.org/blogs/security/2014/05/nuke-exercises/.

———. "Rumors about Nuclear Weapons in Crimea." Strategic Security (blog), Federation of American Scientists, December 18, 2014, https://fas.org/blogs/security/2014/12/crimea/.

Kristensen, Hans M., Alicia Godsberg, and Jonathan Garbose. "Ukraine Special Weapons." Federation of American Scientists. Accessed January 6, 2020. https://fas.org/nuke/guide/ukraine/.

Kristensen, Hans M., and Matt Korda. "Russian Nuclear Forces, 2019." Bulletin of the Atomic Scientists 75, no. 2 (2019): 73–84. https://doi.org/10.1080/00963402.2019.1580891.

———. "Status of World Nuclear Forces." Federation of American Scientists, updated May 2019. https://fas.org/issues/nuclear-weapons/status-world-nuclear-forces/.

Kristensen, Hans M., and Robert S. Norris. "Russian Nuclear Forces, 2014." Bulletin of the Atomic Scientists70, no. 2 (2014): 75–85. https://doi.org/10.1177/0096340214523565.

———. "Russian Nuclear Forces, 2015." Bulletin of the Atomic Scientists 71, no. 3 (2015): 84–97, https://doi.org/10.1177/0096340215581363.

———. "U.S. Nuclear Forces, 2014." Bulletin of the Atomic Scientists 70, no. 1 (2014): 85–93. https://doi.org/10.1177/0096340213516744.

———. "Worldwide Deployments of Nuclear Weapons, 2014." Bulletin of the Atomic Scientists 70, no. 5(2014): 96–108. https://doi.org/10.1177/0096340214547619.

Kroenig, Matthew. "Data Appendices: Nuclear Superiority and the Balance of Resolve: Explaining Nuclear Crisis Outcomes." January 1, 2012.

———. "Nuclear Superiority and the Balance of Resolve: Explaining Nuclear Crisis Outcomes." International Organization 67, no. 1 (Winter 2013): 141–171.

Lake, Eli. "Exclusive: Key General Splits with Obama over Ukraine." Daily Beast, April 11, 2014, updated July 12, 2017. https://www.thedailybeast.com/exclusive-key-general-splits-with-obama-over-ukraine.The RuSSiAN iNvASioN of The CRimeAN PeNiNSulA, 2014–2015 43

Lake, Eli, and Christopher Dickey. "U.S. Spies Said No Russian Invasion of Ukraine—Putin Disagreed." Daily Beast, February 28, 2014, updated July 12, 2017. https://www.thedailybeast.com/us-spies-said-no-russian-invasion-of-ukraineputin-disagreed.

"Low Expectations at the Eastern Partnership Summit." Stratfor, November 27, 2013. http://www.stratfor.com/analysis/low-expectations-eastern-partnership-summit.

MacFarquhar, Neil. "Putin Says He Weighed Nuclear Alert over Crimea." New York Times, March 16, 2015.https://www.nytimes.com/2015/03/16/world/europe/putin-says-he-weighed-nuclear-alert-overcrimea.html.

Magocsi, Paul Robert. History of Ukraine—The Land and Its Peoples. Toronto: University of TorontoPress, 2010.

"Major Russian Exercises Conducted since 2014 in Its European Territory and Adjacent Areas." EuropeanLeadership Network, February, 2016. https://www.europeanleadershipnetwork.org/wp-content/uploads/2017/10/Major-Russian-exercises-TABLE_ELN.pdf.

Marshall, Monty G. "Authority Trends, 1946–2013: Russia." Center for Systemic Peace, 2014. http://www.systemicpeace.org/polity/rus2.htm.

———. "Authority Trends, 1946–2013: United States." Center for Systemic Peace, 2014. http://www.systemicpeace.org/polity/usa2.htm.

McPhedran, Charles. "Russia Takes Charge of Crimea's Military Bases and Officers; Ukraine Pulling out Its Troops from the Region." USA Today, March 20, 2014. https://advance.lexis.com/api/ document?collection=news&id=urn:contentItem:5 BSN-WNK1-DYRR-9343-00000-00&context=1516831.

Medetsky, Anatoly. "Deal Struck on Gas, Black Sea Fleet." Moscow Times, April 22, 2010. https://web.archive.org/web/20100423073455/http://www.themoscowtimes.com/business/article/deal-struck-ongas-black-sea-fleet/404501.html.

Meier, Oliver. "The Ukraine Crisis and Control of Weapons of Mass Destruction: Impacts on GermanArms Control Objectives." SWP Comments 30 (June 2014): 1–7. https://www.swp-berlin.org/fileadmin/contents/products/comments/2014C30_mro.pdf.

Menon, Rajan, and Eugene Rumer. Conflict in Ukraine: The Unwinding of the Post-Cold War Order. Boston:MIT Press, 2015.

"The Military Doctrine of the Russian Federation." From President of the Russian Federation website, February 5, 2010. Carnegie Endowment. https://carnegieendowment.org/files/2010russia_military_doctrine.pdf.

Miller, Daniel. "Ukraine's New Defence Minister Pledges to Retake Crimea Promising a 'Victory Parade'in the Key City of Sevastopol." Daily Mail, July 4, 2014. https://www.dailymail.co.uk/news/article-2680722/Ukraines-new-defence-minister-pledges-retake-Crimea-promising-victory-parade-keycity-Sevastopol.html.44 THE JOHNS HOPKINS UNIVERSITY APPLIED PHYSICS LABORATORY

Ministry of Foreign Affairs. "Statement by the Russian Ministry of Affairs Regarding the Situation in Ukraine." Ministry of Foreign Affairs of the Russia Federation, February 19, 2014. https://web.archive.org/web/20200107205338/https://

www.mid.ru/en/foreign_policy/news/-/asset_publisher/cKNonkJE02Bw/content/id/75606.

Moore, Thomas C. "The Role of Nuclear Weapons during the Crisis in Ukraine." Working paper at The Nuclear Implications of the Ukrainian Crisis: A Seminar at the Fondation pour la Recherche Stratégique (FRS), Paris, The Lugar Center, July 29, 2014. http://www.thelugarcenter.org/newsroom-tlcexperts-8.html.

Nikolsky, Alexey. "Russia Holds Military Drills to repel Nuclear Strike," RT, published May 8, 2014, updated May 10, 2014. https://web.archive.org/web/20190908110730/https://www.rt.com/ news/157644-putin-drills-rocket-launch/.

Norris, Robert S. "The Soviet Nuclear Archipelago." Arms Control Today 22, no. 1 (January/February 1992):24–31. https://www.jstor.org/stable/23624674.

Obama, Barack. "Executive Order—Blocking Property of Additional Persons Contributing to theSituation in Ukraine." Office of the Press Secretary, The White House, March 17, 2014. https://obamawhitehouse.archives.gov/the-press-office/2014/03/17/executive-order-blocking-propertyadditional-persons-contributing-situat.

———. "Executive Order—Blocking Property of Certain Persons Contributing to the Situation in Ukraine." Office of the Press Secretary, The White House, March 6, 2014. https://obamawhitehouse.archives.gov/the-press-office/2014/03/06/executive-order-blocking-property-certain-persons-contributing-situation.

———. "The President's News Conference with President Enrique Peña Nieto of Mexico and Prime Minister Stephen J. Harper of Canada in Toluca, Mexico." Online by Gerhard Peters and John T. Woolley, TheAmerican Presidency Project, February 19, 2014, https://www.presidency.ucsb.edu/node/305148.

———. "Statement by the President on Ukraine." The White House, Office of the Press Secretary, February 28, 2014. https://

obamawhitehouse.archives.gov/the-press office/2014/02/28/statementpresident-ukraine.

Oliphant, Roland, Bruno Waterfield, and Peter Foster. "Russia Risks New Cold War, West Warns asPutin Prepares to Swallow Crimea." Telegraph, March 17, 2014. https://www.telegraph.co.uk/news/worldnews/europe/ukraine/10704117/Russia-risks-new-Cold-War-West-warns-as-Putin-preparesto-swallow-Crimea.html.

O'Malley, Nick. "Kremlin 'Invited to Invade'; Ukraine - Crimean Crisis - U.S. Threatens Russian Officials and Banks with Asset Freezes." Sydney Morning Herald, March 5, 2014. https://advance.lexis.com/api/document?collection=news&id=urn:contentItem:5BN9-H361-F0J6-J3W6-00000-00&context=1516831.

Partition Treaty on the Status and Conditions of the Black Sea Fleet. May 1997, archived September 15, 2015. https://web.archive.org/web/20150915153020/https://en.wikisource.org/wiki/Partition_Treaty_on_the_Status_and_Conditions_of_the_Black_Sea_Fleet.The RuSSiAN iNvASioN of The CRimeAN PeNiNSulA, 2014–2015 45

"Polity IV Country Report 2010: Russia." Center for Systemic Peace, 2010. http://www.systemicpeace.org/polity/Russia2010.pdf.

Rachman, Gideon. "The Nuclear Gun Is Back on the Table." Financial Times, November 17, 2014. https://advance.lexis.com/api/document?collection=news&id=urn:contentItem:5DMB-4TT1-F039-61V0-00000-00&context=1516831.

Resneck, Jacob, and Kim Hjelmgaard. "Both Sides Defiant in 'Biggest Crisis in Europe of 21st Century'; Russians Set an Ultimatum; U.S. Warns Again." USA Today, March 4, 2014. https://advance.lexis.com/api/document?collection=news&id=urn:contentItem:5BN8-H871-JC8N-K1YD-00000-00&context=1516831.

Rooker, Kelly, and James Scouras. Nuclear Crisis Outcomes: Winning, Uncertainty, and the Nuclear Balance. National

Security Report NSAD-R-18-030. Laurel, MD: Johns Hopkins University Applied Physics Laboratory, 2019.

Rosefielde, Steven. The Kremlin Strikes Back: Russia and the West after Crimea's Annexation. New York:Cambridge University Press, 2017.

"Russia." The World Factbook. Washington, DC: Central Intelligence Agency, archived December 30, 2014.https://web.archive.org/web/20141213070624/https://www.cia.gov/library//publications/the-worldfactbook/geos/rs.html.

"Russia, Belarus, Kazakhstan Sign Pact." UPI, November 19, 2011. https://upi.com/3230208.

"Russia Not to Deploy Units of Strategic Missile Forces in Crimea: Commander." Sputnik News, December 16, 2014, archived February 14, 2015. https://web.archive.org/web/20150214232041/http://sputniknews.com/military/20141216/1015893432.html.

"Russia Offers Ukraine Major Economic Assistance." BBC News, December 17, 2013, archived April 6, 2014.https://web.archive.org/web/20140406083526/http://www.bbc.co.uk/news/world-europe-25411118.

"Russia Says Has Right to Deploy Nuclear Weapons in Crimea: Report." Reuters, March 11, 2015. https://www.reuters.com/article/us-russia-crimea-nuclear/russia-says-has-right-to-deploy-nuclear-weaponsin-crimea-report-idUSKBN0M710N20150311.

"The Russian President Gave His Reasons for the Annexation of a Region of Ukraine." Prague Post, March18, 2014. http://praguepost.com/eu-news/37854-full-text-of-putin-s-speech-on-crimea.

Schmemann, Serge. "Russia Votes to Void Cession of Crimea to Ukraine." New York Times, May 22, 1992.http://www.nytimes.com/1992/05/22/world/russia-votes-to-void-cession-of-crimea-to-ukraine.html.

Schneider, Mark B. "Escalate to De-escalate." Proceedings 143, no. 2 (February 2017). https://www.usni.org/magazines/proceedings/2017-02/escalate-de-escalate.

Sharkov, Damien. "Putin Issues 'Nuclear Powers' Warning over Sanctions." Newsweek, October 16, 2014., https://www.newsweek.com/putin-warns-careless-west-nuclear-threat-277867.

Singer, J. David, Stuart Bremer, and John Stuckey. "Capability Distribution, Uncertainty, and Major Power War, 1820-1965." In Peace, War, and Numbers, edited by Bruce Russett, 19–48. Beverly Hills: Sage, 1972.46 THE JOHNS HOPKINS UNIVERSITY APPLIED PHYSICS LABORATORY

Sinovets, Polina. The Nuclear Element in Russia's Asymmetric Warfare Strategies. Policy Memo No. 404.Washington, DC: PONARS Eurasia, December 2015. http://www.ponarseurasia.org/sites/default/files/policy-memos-pdf/Pepm404_Sinovets_Dec2015_0.pdf.

Situation of Human Rights in the Temporarily Occupied Autonomous Republic of Crimea and the City of Sevastopol (Ukraine). Geneva: Office of the United Nations High Commissioner for Human Rights,2017. https://www.ohchr.org/Documents/Countries/UA/Crimea2014_2017_EN.pdf.

Smith-Spark, Laura, Alla Eshchenko, and Emma Burrows. "Russia Was Ready to Put Nuclear Forces on Alert over Crimea, Putin Says." CNN, March 16, 2015. https://www.cnn.com/2015/03/16/europe/russia-putin-crimea-nuclear/index.html.

Soldatkin, Vladimir, and Pavel Polityuk. "Russia Tightens Customs Rules to Force Ukraine into Union."Reuters, August 15, 2013. https://www.reuters.com/article/russia-ukraine-customs/russia-tightenscustoms-rules-to-force-ukraine-into-union-idUSL6N0GG17S20130815.

Sorokowski, Andrew D. "Treaty on Friendship, Cooperation, and Partnership between Ukraine and the Russian Federation."

Harvard Ukrainian Studies 20 (1996): 319–329. https://www.jstor.org/stable/41036701.

Specter, Michael. "Setting Past Aside, Russia and Ukraine Sign Friendship Treaty." New York Times, June 1, 1997. http://www.nytimes.com/1997/06/01/world/setting-past-aside-russia-and-ukraine-sign-friendship-treaty.html.

Steinhauer, Jennifer, and David M. Herszenhorn. "Defying Obama, Many in Congress Press to Arm Ukraine." New York Times, June 11, 2015. https://www.nytimes.com/2015/06/12/world/europe/defying-obama-many-in-congress-press-to-arm-ukraine.html.

Stoltenberg, Jens. "Press Conference by NATO Secretary General Jens Stoltenberg following the Meeting of the NATO-Ukraine Commission." North Atlantic Treaty Organization, May 13, 2015. https://www.nato.int/cps/en/natohq/opinions_119430.htm.

Subtelny, Orest. Ukraine: A History. Toronto: University of Toronto Press, 1988. Sullivan, Tim, and Yuras Karmanau. "Crimea Referendum Vote on Joining Russia Scheduled for March 16." Huffington Post, March 6, 2014, archived March 8, 2014. https://web.archive.org/web/20140308105645/http://www.huffingtonpost.com/2014/03/06/crimea-referendum-russia_n_4910096.html.

Support for the Sovereignty, Integrity, Democracy, and Economic Stability of Ukraine Act of 2014, H.R. 4152, 113th Cong. (2014). https://www.congress.gov/bill/113th-congress/house-bill/4152.

"Table of Global Nuclear Weapons Stockpiles, 1945–2002." In Archive of Nuclear Data. NRDC. ArchivedJuly 14, 2012. https://web.archive.org/web/20120714033315/http:/www.nrdc.org/nuclear/nudb/datab19.asp.

Tan, Su-Lin. "Russian Analyst Urges Nuclear Attack on Yellowstone National Park and San Andreas FaultLine." Sunday Morning Herald, March 31, 2015. https://www.smh.com.au/world/

russian-analyst-urgesnuclear-attack-on-yellowstone-national-park-and-san-andreas-fault-line-20150331-1mbl14.html.The RuSSiAN iNvASioN of The CRimeAN PeNiNSulA, 2014–2015 47

Tayler, Jeffrey. "Putin's Nuclear Option." Foreign Policy, September 4, 2014. https://foreignpolicy.com/2014/09/04/putins-nuclear-option/.

" 'There Was No Quorum': Crimean Lawmaker Calls Vote to Join Russia Flawed." RFE/RL, March 6, 2014.https://www.rferl.org/a/interview-crimea-vote-ukraine-russia/25288146.html.

"Timeline: Key Events in Ukraine." USA Today, March 6, 2014, updated March 19, 2014. https://www.usatoday.com/story/news/nation-now/2014/03/06/ukraine-russia-timeline-obama/6127545/.

Trenin, Dmitri. "Russia's Spheres of Interest, Not Influence." Washington Quarterly 32, no. 4 (2009): 3–22.

Tsygankov, Andrei P. "Russia's International Assertiveness: What Does It Mean for the West?" Problems ofPost-Communism 55, no. 2 (2008): 38–55.

Turchynov, Oleksandr V. "Kyiv's Message to Moscow." New York Times, March 11, 2014. https://www.nytimes.com/2014/03/12/opinion/ukraines-president-rebuffs-russian-imperialism.html?hp&rref=opinion&_r=1.

"Ukraine Crisis: Russian Helicopters Seen 'Flying to Sevastopol.' " Telegraph, February 28, 2014.

"The Ukraine Crisis Timeline." Center for Strategic and International Studies. 2014. Published online the CSIS website and updated throughout the crisis.

"Ukraine Drops EU Plans and Looks to Russia." Al Jazeera, November 21, 2013. http://www.aljazeera.com/news/europe/2013/11/ukraine-drops-eu-plans-looks-russia-20131121145417227621.html.

"Ukraine Leadership Must Be in 'Good Shape' for Ties, Says Russian PM-Ifax." Reuters, February 20, 2014.https://www.reuters.com/article/ukraine-russia-medvedev/ukraine-leadership-must-be-in-goodshape-for-ties-says-russian-pm-ifax-idUSL6N0LP1VE20140220.

"Ukraine, Russia Should Develop Cross-Border and Inter-Regional Cooperation—Yanukovych." InterfaxUkraine, December 17, 2013. https://en.interfax.com.ua/news/general/182398.html.

"Ukraine Seeking Observer Status in Eurasian Economic Union—Yanukovych." Interfax-Ukraine, December 19, 2013. https://en.interfax.com.ua/news/general/182869.html.

Ukraine Support Act, H.R. 4278, 113th Cong. (2014). https://www.congress.gov/bill/113th-congress/

house-bill/4278.

"Ukraine Unrest: Protesters Storm Regional Offices." BBC News, January 24, 2014. https://www.bbc.com/news/world-europe-25876807.

UN (United Nations) General Assembly. "Annex to the Letter Dated 7 November 2003 from the PermanentRepresentative of Ukraine to the United Nations Addressed to the Secretary-General." Fifty-eighth session, Third Committee, A/C.3/58/9, November 7, 2003, archived March 13, 2017. https://web.archive.org/web/20170313040724/http://repository.un.org/bitstream/handle/11176/246001/A_C.3_58_9-EN.pdf.

"United States." The World Factbook. Washington, DC: Central Intelligence Agency, archived December 30, 2014. https://web.archive.org/web/20141230055155/https://www.cia.gov/library/publications/the-world-factbook/geos/us.html.48 THE JOHNS HOPKINS UNIVERSITY APPLIED PHYSICS LABORATORY

UN OCHA (United Nations Office for the Coordination of Humanitarian Affairs). Ukraine: SituationUpdate No. 7 as of August 14, 2015. Geneva: UN OCHA, August 14, 2015.

https://reliefweb.int/sites/reliefweb.int/files/resources/ocha_ukraine_situation_update_number_7_14_august_2015.pdf.

UNSC (United Nations Security Council). Fiftieth Year, 3514th Meeting, S/PV.3514, April 11, 1995. https://undocs.org/pdf?symbol=en/S/PV.3514.

"U.S., Britain, EU Warn against Russian War on Ukraine." Messenger, March 3, 2014. https://advance.lexis.com/api/document?collection=news&id=urn:contentItem:5BN8-H5P1-JB1X-W1V9-00000-00&context=1516831.

U.S. Department of State. Country Reports on Human Rights Practices for 2018: Ukraine 2018 Human RightsReport. Washington, DC: Bureau of Democracy, Human Rights and Labor, March 13, 2019. https://www.state.gov/wp-content/uploads/2019/03/UKRAINE-2018-HUMAN-RIGHTS-REPORT.pdf.

———. "U.S. Government Statement of Concern about Arrest of Former Prime Minister Yulia Tymoshenko."Embassy of the United States. August 6, 2011. Archived January 6, 2016. https://web.archive.org/web/20160106072352/http://ukraine.usembassy.gov/government-statement-tymoshenko.html.

USSTRATCOM Public Affairs. "Global Lightning 14," US Strategic Command, May 11, 2014. https://web.archive.org/web/20140515132156/http://www.stratcom.mil/news/2014/494/Global_Lightning_14.

Vasovic, Aleksandar, and Gabriela Baczynska. "Acknowledging Defeat, Ukraine Pulls Troops from Crimea." Reuters, March 24, 2014. https://www.reuters.com/article/us-ukraine-crisis-crimea-base/acknowledging-defeat-ukraine-pulls-troops-from-crimea-idUSBREA2N09J20140324.

Verkhovna Rada of Ukraine. "Declaration of State Sovereignty of Ukraine." July 16, 1990.

———. "Verkhovna Rada of Ukraine Resolution on Declaration of Independence of Ukraine." August 24, 1991.

"Vladimir Putin Signs Russia's Annexation of Crimea Into Law." NBC News, March 21, 2014. https://www.nbcnews.com/storyline/ukraine-crisis/vladimir-putin-signs-russias-annexation-crimea-law-n58526.

VOA News. "A Brief History of Crimea." Voice of America, February 27, 2014. https://www.voanews.com/europe/brief-history-crimea.

Walker, Shaun. "Ukraine's EU Trade Deal Will Be Catastrophic, Says Russia." Guardian, September 22, 2013. https://www.theguardian.com/world/2013/sep/22/ukraine-european-union-trade-russia.

"Warning Shots Fired at Ukrainian Troops in Crimea—Video." Video.Guardian, March 4, 2014.https://www.theguardian.com/world/video/2014/mar/04/warning-shots-fired-ukrainian-troops-crimea-video.

Watts, Joseph, and Will Stewart. "Ukraine 'Invaded' as Armed Men Seize Key Sites in Crimea." Evening Standard, February 28, 2014. https://www.questia.com/newspaper/1G1-360115381/ukraine-invaded-as-armed-men-seize-key-sites-in.

"West Struggles for Any Traction over Ukraine." New Zealand Herald. March 5, 2014. https://advance.lexis.com/api/document?collection=news&id=urn:contentItem:5BNB-3XT1-JCBG-G3RF-00000-00&context=1516831.

Kobzova, J. (2011) "Great Power Management Without Great Powers? The Russian-Georgian War of 2008 and Global Police/Political Order", in A. Astrov (eds.) The Great Power (mis)Management, The Russian-Georgian War and its Implications for Global Political Order, (UK: Ashgate Publishing Limited), pp. 79-102.

Baldwin, D. A. and Pape R. A. (1998) "Evaluating Economic Sanctions", International Security, 23(2): 189-198.

Bebler, A. (2015) "Crimea and the Russian-Ukrainian Conflict," Romanian Journal of European Affairs, 15(1): 35-54.

Blanc, J. and Weiss, A. S. (2019) "U.S. Sanctions on Russia: Congress Should Go Back to Fundamentals," Carnegie Endowment for International Peace",3 Nisan 2019, <https://carnegieendowment.org/2019/04/03/u.s.-sanctionson-russia-congress-should-go-back-to-fundamentals-pub-78755>, (07 Eylül2019).

Brunat, E. (2016) "Where goes Russia? The risks of a new continental divide" B. Dallago, G. Guri and J. McGowan (eds.) A Global Perspective on the European Economic Crisis, (Abingdon, Oxfordshire: Routledge), pp. 241-258.

Buchet de Neilly, Y. (2003) "The multi-pillar issue of economic sanctions against Serbia," in M. Knodt and S. Princen (eds.) Understanding the European Union's External Relations, (London: Routledge), pp. 92-106.

Carlsson, M. Oxenstierna, S. and Weissmann, M. (2015) "China and Russia – A Study on Cooperation, Competition and Distrust", June 2015,<https://www.foi.se/rest-api/report/FOI-R--4087--SE>, (07 Eylül 2019).

Carroll, J. J. (2014) "This is Not about Europe: Reflections on Ukraine's EuroMaidan Revolution", Perspectives of Europe, 44(1): 8-15.

Council Decision 2014/145/CFSP of 17 March 2014 concerning restrictive measures in respect of actions undermining or threatening the territorialintegrity, sovereignty and independence of Ukraine,<https://eurlex.europa.eu/legalcontent/en/TXT/?qid=1521625455688&uri=CELEX:02014D0145-20171121>, (31 Ocak 2019).

Council of the European Union (2019) "Sanctions: how and when the EU adopts restrictive measures",<https://www.consilium.europa.eu/en/policies/sanctions/>, (31 Ocak 2019).

Council of the European Union (2014) "3309th Council Meeting, Foreign Affairs," Press Release 8763/14,<https://www.consilium.europa.eu/media/28449/142228.pdf>, (30 Ocak 2019).

Department of the Treasury (2016) "Ukraine/Russia-related sanctions program," Office of Foreign Assets Control, U.S. Department of the Treasury,<https://www.treasury.gov/resourcecenter/sanctions/Programs/Documents/ukraine.pdf>, (31 Ocak 2019).

De Vries, A. (2002) "European Union sanctions against the Federal Republic of Yugoslavia (1998-2000): A special exercise in targeting", D. Cortright, G.A. Lopez (eds.) Smart sanctions: targeting economic statecraft, (UK:Rowman & Littlefield Publishers, Lanham), pp. 87-108.

De Wilde d'Estmael, T. (1998) Political dimension of the external economic relations of European Community: Sanctions and economic incentives as foreign policy means (La dimension politique des relations économiques extérieures de la communauté européenne. Sanctions et incitants économiques comme moyens de politique étrangère), (Bruxelles, Etablissements Emile Bruylant).

Doxey, M. (1983) "International Sanctions in Theory and Practice," Case Western Reserve Journal of International Law, 15(2): 273-288.

EU Delegation to the Russian Federation (2018) "EU restrictive measures in response to the crisis in Ukraine", <https://eeas.europa.eu/sites/eeas/files/eu_restrictive_measures_in_response_to_crisis_in_ukraine_en.pdf>, (31 Ocak 2019).

European Commission (2019) "Trade policy, Countries and Regions, Russia",<https://ec.europa.eu/trade/policy/countries-and regions/countries/russia/>,(07 Eylül 2019).

European Commission (2013) "Third Eastern Partnership Summit, Vilnius 28- 29 November 2013", Press Release,

<http://europa.eu/rapid/pressrelease_IP-13-1169_en.htm>, (30 Ocak 2019).

European Council (2018) "European Council conclusions 13-14 December 2018", <https://www.consilium.europa.eu/media/37535/14-euco-finalconclusions-en.pdf>, (31 Ocak 2019).

European Parliament (2017) "Russia's and the EU's sanctions: economic and trade effects, compliance and the way forward," Directorate General for External Policies, Committee on International Trade,<http://www.europarl.europa.eu/RegData/etudes/STUD/2017/603847/EXPO_STU(2017)603847_EN.pdf>, (07 Eylül 2019).

European Parliament (2017b) "Parliamentary Questions: Renewal of sanctions against Russia: lossess of billions of euros for the 'Made in Italy' sector",<http://www.europarl.europa.eu/doceo/document/E-8-2017-004795_EN.html>, (07 Eylül 2019).

European Parliament (2016), "Sanctions Over Ukraine, Impact on Russia," Policy Brief March 2016, <http://www.europarl.europa.eu/EPRS/EPRS-Briefing-579084-Sanctions-over-Ukraine-impact-Russia-FINAL.pdf>, (31 Ocak 2019).

Executive Order 13685 of December 19, 2014, Presidential Documents, Federal Register Vol. 79, No. 247, <https://www.treasury.gov/resourcecenter/sanctions/Programs/Documents/ukraine_eo4.pdf>, (09 Şubat 2019).

Flowe Jr, B H. (1980) "An Overview of Export Controls on Transfer of Technology to the U.S.S.R. in Light of Soviet Intervention in Afghanistan," North Carolina Journal of International Law and Commercial Regulation, UNC School of Law, 5(3): 555-573.

Galtung, J. (1967) "On the Effects of the International Economic Sanctions: With Examples from the Case of Rhodesia," World Politics, 19(3): 378-416. Gould-Davies, N. (2018) Economic effects and political impacts: Assessing Western sanctions on Russia," Bank of Finland, BOFIT, Institute for Economics in Transition,<https://helda.helsinki.fi/bof/bitstream/handle/123456789/15832/bpb0818.pdf?sequence=1>, (07 Eylül 2019).

Gurvich, E. and I. Prilepskiy (2015), "The impact of financial sanctions on the Russian economy", Russian Journal of Economics, 1: 359-385.

Hovi, J. Huseby, R. and Sprinz, D. F. (2005) "When Do (Imposed) Economic Sanctions Work?", World Politics, 57(4): 479-499.

Hufbauer, G. C. Schott, J.J. Elliott, K. A. and Oegg, B. (2007) Economic Sanctions Reconsidered, 3rd Edition, (Washington DC: Peterson Institute for International Economics).

Ikenberry, J. G. (2014) "From Hegemony to the Balance of Power: The Rise of China and American Grand Strategy in East Asia", International Journal of Korean Unification Studies, 23(2): 41-63.

Kaempfer, W. H. and Lowenberg, A. D. (2007) "The Political Economy of Economic Sanctions", Handbook of Defence Economics, 2: 867-911.

Kennan Cable (2017) "U.S. Sanctions and Western Coordination on Russia Policy" December 2017,<https://www.wilsoncenter.org/sites/default/files/kennan_cable_29_-

_tolksdorf.pdf>, (07 Eylül 2019).

Kholodilin, K. and Netsunajev, A. (2016) "Crimea and Punishment: The Impact of Sanctions on Russian and European Economies", Deutsches Institut für Wirtschaftsforschung DISCUSSION PAPERS, No. 1569.

Kirshner, J. (1998) "Political Economy in Security Studies after the Cold War", Review of International Political Economy, 5(1): 64-91.

Korhonen, I. Simola, H. and Solanko, L. (2018) "Sanctions, counter-sanctions and Russia – Effects on economy, trade and finance", Bank of Finland, BOFIT, Institute for Economics in Transition, <https://helda.helsinki.fi/bof/bitstream/handle/123456789/15510/bpb0418.p df?sequence=1>, (03 Şubat 2019).

Korteweg, R. (2018) "Energy as a tool of foreign policy of authoritarian states, in particular Russia," European Parliament Committee on Foreign Affairs., Directorate-General for External Policies of the Union,<http://www.europarl.europa.eu/RegData/etudes/STUD/2018/603868/EXPO_STU(2018)603868_EN.pdf>, (28 Ocak 2019).

Kremlin (2019) "Joint news conference with Italian Prime Minister Giuseppe Conte", President of Russia,<http://en.kremlin.ru/events/president/news/page/14>, (07 Eylül 2019).Lo, B. (2015) Russia and the New World Disorder, (London: Chatham House).

Morello, C. Constable, P. and Faiola, A. (2014) "Crimeans vote to break away from Ukraine, join Russia", 16 March, 2014,<https://www.washingtonpost.com/world/2014/03/16/ccec2132-acd4-11e3-a06a-e3230a43d6cb_story.html?utm_term=.1b3054f2b18d>, (30 Ocak 2019).

Neuenkirchn, M. and Neumeier, F. (2015) "The Impact of UN and US Economic Sanctions on GDP Growth," European Journal of Political Economy, 40: 110-125.

North Atlantic Treaty Organisation (NATO) (2014) "Doorstep statement by NATO Secretary General Anders Fogh Rasmussen before the meetings of the North Atlantic Council and the NATO-Ukraine Commission", 2 March 2014, <https://www.nato.int/cps/en/natolive/opinions_107663.htm>, (30 Ocak 2019).

Van Bergeijk, P.A.G. (1989) "Success and Failure of Economic Sanctions", KYKLOS, 42: 385-404.

Jentleson, B. W. (2000) "Economic Sanctions and Post-Cold War Conflicts: Challenges for Theory and Policy," National Research Council (eds.) International Conflict Resolution After the Cold War, (Washington DC: The National Academies Press), pp. 123-177.

Lacy, D. and Niou, E. M. S. (2004) "A Theory of Economic Sanctions and Issue Linkage: The Roles of Preferences, Information, and Threats," The Journal of Politics, 66(1): 25-42.

Pape, R. A. (1997) "Why Economic Sanctions Do Not Work", International Security Journal, 22(2): 90-136.

Paul, A. (2015) "Crimea one year after Russian annexation", 15 March 2015, <http://aei.pitt.edu/62987/1/pub_5432_crimea_one_year_after_russian_anne xation.pdf>, (07 Eylül 2019).

Perovic, J. (2017) Cold War Energy: A Transnational History of Soviet Oil and Gas, (UK: Palgrave Macmillan).

Portela, C. (2010) European Union Sanctions and Foreign Policy: When and why do they work?, (London: Routledge, Taylor and Francis Group).

Presidium of the USSR Supreme Soviet (1954) "Meeting of the Presidium of the Supreme Soviet of the Union of Soviet Socialist Republics", <https://digitalarchive.wilsoncenter.org/document/119638>, (03 Şubat2019).

Rappeport, A. and MacFarquhar, N. (2017) "Trump Imposes New Sanctions on Russia Over Ukraine Incursion", 20 June 2017,<https://www.nytimes.com/2017/06/20/world/europe/united-statessanctions-russia-ukraine.html>, (29 Ocak 2019).

Reisman, M. W. and Stevick, D. L. (1998) "The Applicability of International Law Standards to United Nations Economic Sanctions Programmes", European Journal of International Law, 9: 86-141.

"Russian Forces Occupy Strategic Facilities in Crimea," The Ukraine Crisis Timeline, February 28, 2014, <http://ukraine.csis.org/crimea.htm#3>, (30 Ocak 2019).

Russell, M. (2018) "Sanctions Over Ukraine, Impact on Russia," European Parliament Research Service, <http://www.europarl.europa.eu/RegData/etudes/BRIE/2018/614665/EPRS_BRI(2018)614665_EN.pdf>, (03 Şubat 2019).

Russell, M. (2018b) "EU sanctions: A key foreign and security policy instrument," European Parliament Research Service, <http://www.europarl.europa.eu/RegData/etudes/BRIE/2018/621870/EPRS_

BRI(2018)621870_EN.pdf>, (07 Eylül 2019).

Russell, M. (2016) "Sanctions Over Ukraine, Impact on Russia," European Parliament Research Service, <http://www.europarl.europa.eu/EPRS/EPRSBriefing-579084-Sanctions-over-Ukraine-impact-Russia-FINAL.pdf>, (07 Eylül 2019).

Sabitova, N. and Shavaleyeva, C. (2015), "Oil and Gas Revenues of the Russian Federation: Trends and Prospects," Procedia Economics and Finance, 27: 423-428.

Schellinck, P. (2018) "EU prolongs sanctions over actions against Ukraine," European News Agency, 18 March 2018, <https://www.european-newsagency.de/special_interest/eu_prolongs_sanctions_over_actions_against_kraine-70556/>, (31 Ocak 2019).

Sheftalovich, Z. (2018) "Putin accuses Ukrainian president of provoking confrontation to boost popularity," Politico, 28 November 2018, <https://www.politico.eu/article/russian-president-vladimir-putin-accusesukrainian-leader-petro-poroshenko-of-provoking-kerch-strait-crisis-toboost-popularity/>, (28 Ocak 2019).

Shevtsova, L. et al. (2014), "The Maidan and Beyond," Journal of Democracy, 25(3): 74-82.

Smeets, M. (2018) "Can Economic Sanctions Be Effective," Staff Working Paper ERSD, World Trade Organisation, Economic Research and Statistics Division, <https://www.wto.org/english/res_e/reser_e/ersd201803_e.pdf>, (28 Ocak 2019).

Smith, B. (2018) "Sanctions against Russia – in brief," Commons Library Briefing, No CBP 8284, <http://researchbriefings.files.parliament.uk/documents/CBP-8284/CBP-

8284.pdf>, (03 Şubat 2019).

Sospedra, J. T. (2018) "Relations between USA-Russia: a new cold war? The moment of Trump," Instituto Español de Estudios Estratégicos, <http://www.ieee.es/en/Galerias/fichero/docs_opinion/2018/DIEEEO04- 2018_Relaciones_EEUU-Rusia_Torres_Sospedra_ENGLISH.pdf>, (01 Şubat 2019).

The White House (2014) "Statement by the President on Ukraine," Office of the Press Secretary, 20 March, 2014, <https://obamawhitehouse.archives.gov/the-pressoffice/2014/03/20/statement-president-ukraine>, (30 Ocak 2019).

The White House (2014b) "Executive Order – Blocking Property of Additional Persons Contributing to the Situation in Ukraine," Office of the Press Secretary, 20 March 2014, <https://obamawhitehouse.archives.gov/thepress-office/2014/03/20/executive-order-blocking-property-additionalpersons-contributing-situat>, (05 Şubat 2019).

Trenin, D. (2014) "The Ukraine Crisis and the Presumption of Great-Power Rivalry," Carnegie Moscow Center,<https://carnegieendowment.org/files/ukraine_great_power_rivalry2014.pdf>, (29 Ocak 2019).

Tyll, L. Pernica, K. and Arltova, M. (2018) "The impact of economic sanctions on Russian economy and the RUB/USD exchange rate", Journal of International Studies, 11(1): 21-33. U.S. Department of State, "Ukraine and Russia Sanctions," <https://www.state.gov/e/eb/tfs/spi/ukrainerussia/index.htm>, (30 Ocak 2019).

U.S. Department of State (2018b) "Russia Fact Sheet," Bureau of Economic and Business Affairs, <https://www.state.gov/e/eb/rls/fs/2018/288152.htm>, (30 Ocak 2019).

Valdai Discussion Club Report (2014) "The crisis in Ukraine: Root causes and scenarios for the future," Valdai Discussion Club, <http://vid- 1.rian.ru/ig/valdai/ukraine_eng.pdf>, (30 Ocak 2019).

Wayne Merry, E. (2015) "Dealing with the Ukrainian Crisis: Transatlantic Strategy Dilemmas," Istituto Affari Internazionali, IAI Working Paper, 15∥51.

Weiss, T. G. (1999) "Sanctions as a Foreign Policy Tool: Weighing Humanitarian Impulses," Journal of Peace and Research, 35(5): 499-510.

Welt, C. (2017) "Ukraine: Background and U.S. Policy," Congressional Research Service (CRS Report), 1 November 2017, <https://fas.org/sgp/crs/row/R45008.pdf>, (30 Ocak 2019).

Other sources

Aljazeera (http://www.aljazeera.com/)

British Broadcasting Corporation - BBCNews (http://www.bbc.com/)

Cable News Network - CNN (http://edition.cnn.com/)

Chicago Tribune (http://www.chicagotribune.com/)

European Union (http://europa.eu/)

Fox News (http://www.foxnews.com/)

International Institute for StrategicStudies – IISS (http://www.iiss.org/)

IHS Jane's (http://www.janes.com/)

Kyiv Post (http://www.kyivpost.com/)

North Atlantic Treaty Organization -NATO (http://www.nato.int/)

NBC News (http://www.nbcnews.com/)

Reuters (http://www.reuters.com/)

RT news (https://www.rt.com/news/)

Tass Russian News Agency (http://tass.ru/en)

The Guardian (http://www.theguardian.com/international)

The Independent (http://www.independent.co.uk/)

The Telegraph (http://www.telegraph.co.uk/)

UNIAN Information Agency (http://www.unian.info/)

United Kingdom Parliament (http://www.publications.parliament.uk/)

United Press International - UPI (http://www.upi.com/)

World Affairs Journal (http://worldaffairsjournal.org/)